Signs &
Wonders
Today

Edited by
C. Peter Wagner

Creation House
Strang Communications Company
190 N. Westmonte Drive
Altamonte Springs, FL 32714

Creation House
Strang Communications Company
190 N. Westmonte Drive
Altamonte Springs, FL 32714
(305) 869-5005

Contents

Introduction

Fuller Seminary is going charismatic!''
"Fuller Seminary has declared John Wimber a heretic!''
"Fuller Seminary has legislated against the Holy Spirit!''

These statements and many others equally contradictory and unfounded have been circulating in Christian circles recently. As it has many times since its founding in 1947, Fuller Theological Seminary in Pasadena, California, has once again become a center of theological controversy. And whether the debate revolves around neo-evangelicalism, biblical inerrancy, contextualization of theology, Christian psychology, evangelical feminism or supernatural signs and wonders, the seminary usually finds itself positioned somewhere near the middle, receiving verbal salvos from both the right and left.

The most recent episode was precipitated by the introduction of a new course in the winter quarter of 1982 called MC510, Signs, Wonders and Church Growth. I signed off as the seminary's official professor of record, but I did very little of the actual teaching. Instead, I invited my friend John Wimber, pastor of the Vineyard Christian Fellowship of Anaheim, to do most of the teaching. So far as we know, this was the pioneering effort—the first time a course of this nature was offered in a major accredited seminary.

We did not introduce the course because we thought Fuller

3

Seminary needed another badge of uniqueness, much less to invite a new controversy. We did so basically because the faculty of the School of World Mission, where I teach, felt that God had been giving John Wimber some valuable insights in recent years which would be extremely useful to our students in their ministry in some seventy countries of the world. We had recently been warned by some friends of ours that we were in danger of concentrating so heavily on the behavioral sciences and technology of church growth that we would leave out the sovereign work of the Holy Spirit in world missions. So we asked John to help us readjust our focus on the Holy Spirit.

Little did we imagine that the course, which was taught for four years (1982-1985), would attract as many theology students as missions students. We also had no idea that Robert Walker of *Christian Life* magazine would fly out from Wheaton, Illinois, to attend one of the classes and write a story on it.

Walker was so impressed that he did more than write a story. In a rare editorial switch, he decided to dedicate an entire issue of *Christian Life* to the course. The October 1982 issue came out with a dramatic cover which exclaimed, "MC510 ORIGIN, HISTORY, IMPACT: COULD THIS NUMBER AFFECT YOUR FAITH?" The issue was sold out more rapidly than any other the magazine had published and orders for reprints were so numerous that the first edition of the book you have in your hands was published in 1983 under the title *Signs and Wonders Today*. Fuller's experiment was still in its infancy, but it had already become a center of public attention in the Christian world.

There is no need to tell more of this part of the story, since most of the material in this revised and expanded edition of *Signs and Wonders Today* was included in that October 1982 issue of *Christian Life*, and you can read the story in full. Seminary president David Allan Hubbard explains how the seminary sees its role to experiment with innovations while yet keeping a theological balance. John Wimber and I relate how manifestations of signs and wonders in Vineyard Christian Fellowship sparked interest among seminary professors and students, leading to MC510. Interviews with professors such as Donald McGavran, Dean Gilliland, Glen Barker and Charles Kraft will allow you to see the inner working of their minds on the issue. A number of students tell what MC510 meant to them.

But this revised edition is also expanded. It contains a previously unpublished essay on divine healing by Donald McGavran, founding dean of the Fuller School of World Mission. Eddie Gibbs evaluates John Wimber and the impact he has had over the years, also raising key questions with which the faculty at Fuller Seminary is grappling. Charles Kraft, professor of intercultural studies, tells how God used John Wimber to bring him to a new understanding of what the Christian faith is all about. The material is inspiring and faith-building, as you will see.

Now, back to the seminary.

Because of the public attention that MC510 received, it became different in kind from the other hundreds of courses listed in the seminary catalog. As a seminary conversation piece, accountability for the course to faculty colleagues in other schools became much higher than usual. Fuller Seminary is made up of three separate schools, theology, psychology and world mission, each with its own dean, budget, curriculum and academic degree program. MC510 was a world mission course, but open to students from other schools.

As the course progressed, many students (as well as missions faculty) underwent what we have come to call a "paradigm shift." A paradigm is a mental grid through which we interpret certain segments of reality. People with different paradigms understand the same information in different ways. Most of us at Fuller had a straightline evangelical paradigm concerning supernatural signs and wonders. We believed that they happened in biblical times, but we weren't really sure whether they should happen today. John Wimber, who came from the same theological background and who went through his paradigm shift in the late '70s had already become convinced that they were for today. He was participating in a ministry of miraculous healing in the church he pastored and was prepared to teach seminary students how to understand these phenomena and how to pray effectively for the sick.

Over the four years during which MC510 was taught, many of us began to interpret both personal experiences and biblical data in a different way. While our entire mission faculty was open to this, some turned out to be early adopters, some took a little more time, and some are still wondering how they personally fit into the new paradigm. Through it all there was never a question of personal loyalty or faculty unity on offering the course. Most of the missions faculty attended classes from time to time. All loved and appreciated John Wimber, who was no stranger. He had been an adjunct faculty member since 1975, teaching classes in church growth.

Two of the earliest adopters were Charles Kraft and I. We both began experimenting with what we were learning in the churches we belonged to, Kraft in the Pasadena Covenant Church and I in Lake Avenue Congregational Church. We wanted to see for ourselves whether a ministry of praying for the sick, as taught in MC510, would be acceptable in traditional evangelical churches without causing problems of divisiveness.

Because of the wide publicity in the media, many faculty members began getting telephone calls and letters of concern from their friends both in mainline conciliar churches and in evangelical churches. They asked what was happening to Fuller. They were getting the impression that Fuller was "going charismatic." These pressures also increased over the four years until some theology professors wondered whether the missions faculty could be leading the entire seminary astray. Some imagined that we were training Fuller students to be like the television faith healer types for whom they did not have particularly high appreciation. Attempts were made to improve communications between the two schools, but they were not adequate so the system unfortunately grew hotter and hotter.

The point of eruption came in the spring of 1985 when the issue was raised in a theology faculty meeting. Many of the professors who had previously thought they were the only ones feeling the tensions suddenly found that a good proportion of other faculty members was in the same position. As the discussion progressed, strong feelings emerged, and the faculty decided that from then on no theology student would be awarded academic credit for MC510. They questioned the theological, exegetical, historical and pastoral integrity of the course.

Since this was the first time in the history of Fuller Seminary that something like this had happened, it took a while to sort out the issues and decide how to proceed. Meetings were held, task forces were formed, memos were written, but not much progress was made until Lawrence den Besten arrived as seminary provost in January 1986.

The previous provost, the person in charge of all the academic administration over the three schools, was Glen Barker about whom you will read in this book. Both he and President David Allan Hubbard were supportive of MC510 throughout the whole process, as you will see. But Glen Barker had died suddenly of a heart attack in May 1984 and the provost's office was not occupied at the time of the MC510 crisis. Den Besten immediately took charge of the issue and channeled it in a highly creative direction.

The first step was for the School of World Mission, under the leadership of Dean Paul Pierson, to withdraw MC510 for the 1985-86 academic year. This allowed the provost to set up an all-seminary process without the added pressure of deciding who could or who could not get credit for a particular course.

It was at this point that many public misunderstandings arose. Some of the media reports gave the impression that Fuller had denounced John Wimber or declared him a heretic. Some imagined that Fuller had taken an anti-charismatic position and had turned its back on supernatural healing and signs and wonders. None of this was true. The problem was only MC510. John Wimber began teaching classes in the doctor of ministry program in 1976 and he continues to do so. He began lecturing on signs and wonders in that same program in 1981 and continues to do so. He is respected at Fuller as an internationally known Christian leader, a pastor and a teacher.

The provost then proceeded to name a faculty task force, chaired by theology professor Lewis Smedes, to work through the issues raised by MC510 and to submit a written report to him. Professors from all three schools were included. Joining Smedes from the School of Theology were James Bradley, Colin Brown, Roberta Hestenes, Donald Hagner, Samuel Southard and Russell Spittler. From the School of Psychology were Newton Malony and Hendrika vande Kemp. From the School of World Mission were Arthur Glasser, Paul Hiebert and I.

The task force labored for eight months, doing what many feel a theological seminary ought to do. Controversial issues are bound to arise within any Christian institution which perceives its mission to explore the cutting edges of what the Holy Spirit is currently saying to the churches. We think of ourselves as a community of scholars who come from divergent theological traditions but who adhere to a common evangelical commitment as reflected in the ten clauses of the Fuller Statement of Faith. Those constitute our theological non-negotiables. The statement of faith does not prescribe a certain position on miraculous healings or supernatural signs and wonders. On such issues there is wide tolerance of differing opinions, and this would have applied to MC510 if it had not been for the disproportionate emphasis it had experienced both within and outside the seminary. As one professor put it, "Our problem was too much too soon."

Speaking as an insider, I can report that the task force discussions were open, frank and lively. Paper after paper was written and debated. A special effort was made not to conceal any hidden agendas or to sweep the most controversial issues under the rug. During the first few meetings emotions were high. Fear, anger, suspicion, skepticism and even distrust were evident. But all was bathed in prayer. Not only did the task force pray together, but the separate faculties prayed, the students prayed, and many individuals and groups and entire congregations outside the seminary were praying basically for one thing: that the task force would deliberate under the Lordship of Jesus Christ and thereby listen to what the Holy Spirit was saying to the seminary.

As the months rolled by, it became more and more evident that the prayer was being answered. Discussion became calmer, areas of agreement became broader, trust was built. God healed some strained personal relationships between committee members. As a result, in November 1986 a remarkable 82-page document was delivered to the provost and then accepted by the joint faculty and affirmed with applause and an almost audible sigh of relief.

The document, which carries the title "Ministry and the Miraculous," is remarkable because at the beginning of the process there was no assurance that a group of twelve professors, all holding both doctoral degrees and strong theological convictions, could ever come to a consensus on such a potentially explosive issue. Fuller is a multidenominational seminary. At least forty denominations have five students or more at Fuller and about fifty more have fewer than five. The full-time faculty reflects the spectrum, representing twenty-three different denominations from Assemblies of God to Episcopal, from Presbyterian to Mennonite, from Methodist to Reformed, and much more. Unlike denominational seminaries, Fuller feels a responsibility to address the needs of all the theological traditions represented in the student body with as high a degree of integrity as possible.

The statement wrestles with biblical and theological issues relating to the kingdom of God. It describes how signs and wonders were part of the ministry of the early church. It considers worldview and the reality of the demonic alongside the activities of God in creation and in nature. It recognizes the place of suffering in the Christian life and deals with how miraculous healing is handled pastorally, especially when God does not choose to heal at a particular time. It speaks of the need for feeding the poor and of social justice. It warns against counterfeit miracles and calls for biblical discernment.

Not one of the twelve professors would have written the

document as it appears. Some would have preferred that certain parts be omitted or stated in different language. Others had hoped that certain of their agenda items would be included, but instead they were dropped. But a spirit of mutual respect prevailed and the rights of one another to say what we thought needed to be said were honored and a unanimous consensus was reached.

Where does Fuller Seminary now stand? Here are some items which are now clear:

1. Fuller Seminary believes in the miraculous. No one questions whether God can and does work miraculously. Jesus' miracles are accepted at face value, not allegorized or explained away as they are by some liberal theologians. God's miraculous interventions in human life today are affirmed, although there is some divergence of view as to how frequently we should expect them in our lives or in our churches.

2. Fuller Seminary believes that all the spiritual gifts are in use in the body of Christ today. We do not agree with those who contend that the sign gifts ceased with the apostolic age. We recognize that God does not give all the gifts to all churches, but we encourage the use of all the gifts He gives and we desire to train our students to use whatever gifts they have responsibly.

3. Fuller Seminary is not anti-charismatic. As a multidenominational school we are no more anti-charismatic than anti-Wesleyan or anti-Reformed or anti-Anabaptist or anti-Lutheran or anti-holiness or anti-liturgical. We are evangelical.

4. Fuller Seminary attempts to provide training to men and women who desire to understand the healing ministry and to learn how to pray for the sick more effectively. Samuel Southard offers a course in demonization and mental illness, in which John Wimber is a guest teacher. Colin Brown offers a course in miracles. Cecil Robeck offers a course in spiritual gifts. Newton Malony and Russell Spittler offer a course in healing.

The dean asked Charles Kraft to join with me in designing a new School of World Mission course replacing MC510. We call it MC550, The Ministry of Healing and World Evangelization. As you will see in this book, both Kraft and I are disciples of John Wimber and at least one session of the class is held in Vineyard Christian Fellowship with Wimber teaching. Furthermore, several other professors, drawn from all three schools, deliver relevant lectures from the perspective of their areas of expertise. During the first session of the new course in spring 1987, 150 students enrolled. More than half were from the School of Theology.

There is no question that a new and exciting era has come upon Christianity in the twentieth century. It started with the Pentecostal movement at the beginning of the century, a movement which continues to multiply under God's blessing. It was joined by the charismatic movement soon after mid-century. And now in these latter decades the Spirit is moving in what some of us like to call the third wave where we are seeing the miraculous works of God operating as they have been in the other movements in churches which have not been nor intend to be either Pentecostal or charismatic.

How all of this comes together you will discover as you read the pages which follow. Each stimulating chapter is followed by a series of discussion questions and applications which can be used in group study. My prayer is that God will use this book to help you and your friends become open channels for the wonderful healing and saving power which He desires to pour out to a lost world in these latter days.

A combination of theological balance, personal integrity and openness to the movement of the Holy Spirit is necessary for an evangelical seminary to teach a course like MC510, Signs, Wonders and Church Growth. In this statement the president of Fuller Seminary brings those qualities together with finesse.

1

Hazarding the Risks

by David Allan Hubbard

"The age of miracles is past," one group of Christians asserts. Another claims, "Miracles can be seen nightly at 7:30, except Saturday."

The two extremes seem either obviously presumptuous or based on an inadequate understanding of the Scriptures.

Miracles in Bunches

True, the Bible does contain accounts of numerous miracles, but we must not overlook the fact that these accounts come in bunches. They are not spread evenly through the text. There are the miracles of Genesis 1-2; the whole creation story is alive with miracles. There are signs and wonders by Moses and Joshua in the accounts of the exodus from Egypt and the settlement of Canaan. There are the mighty works of Elijah and Elisha, the sun dial of Hezekiah, the defeat of Sennacherib recorded in the book of Kings. There are the miracles of Jesus and the apostles, signaling the presence of the kingdom.

But between and after these bursts of miraculous power are vast stretches of the biblical period where no such wonders appear. We may conclude from this pattern that God reserves the right to work miracles for His purpose and on His schedule.

Thus these extremes—"no miracles now" or "miracles whenever we program them"—do not seem to reflect a biblical pattern. But finding that pattern—which appears to lie somewhere between the two extremes—and applying it to the life of the churches in our day is no simple task.

Finding a Balance

For thirty-five years at Fuller Seminary we have sought both to teach the tenets of biblical faith as interpreted by the Reformers and to be open to the experiences and contributions of the current movement of the Holy Spirit which came into prominence about the turn of our century. The course taught recently by professors John Wimber and Peter Wagner is an expression of our long-term interest in preserving a biblical balance between the extremes.

Hazarding the risks of this approach to the life of the Spirit is part of what Fuller is prepared to do. Pentecostal excesses have sometimes led to what my parents, who came under the Pentecostal influence in 1923, used to call "wildfire"—an exuberance which resulted in selfish exhibitionism rather than in spiritual ministry to the church.

The risk on the other side is equally dangerous—*powerlessness*. Life frequently puts us in places where we confront the forces of evil and need a power beyond our own. To engage in such conflict with intellectual equipment—doctrine alone, as vital as that is—may not be enough. We need all that the Holy Spirit is in order to cope with the secular, pagan or demonic forces that seek to limit our effectiveness as Christians.

Avoiding Divisiveness

Another risk we have to be willing to hazard is *divisiveness*. Probably no label is pinned more readily on charismatic believers, especially when they are found in non-Pentecostal churches. Scores of pastors have complained to me about the small, but forceful, group of charismatics that has urged other members to seek the Spirit's gifts and has, thus, become "divisive."

I have asked these pastors how they have handled this charismatic "problem." Usually they have stammered out answers like, "Well, you know, I have tried to talk them out of their experiences, straighten out their theology and so on." In extreme cases, the pastor has answered, "I tell them, shape up or ship out.''

When people of charismatic experience are treated that way, the obvious question is, ''Who is responsible for the divisiveness, the enthusiastic charismatic or the pastor?'' Change carries risks. But so does resistance to change. Change in an understanding of the Spirit's work may lead to excessive zeal that advocates ''speaking in tongues'' as the answer to all personal and social problems. But refusing to change may lead to deadly orthodoxy, smug spiritual complacency that assumes, ''We know all truth and are totally satisfied with our level of spiritual maturity.''

The Biblical Pattern

Following the biblical pattern lies at the heart of our educational commitment. We are dedicated to finding out how God has worked in the past and how He is working at present to make His church grow. Who can doubt the role of signs and wonders in establishing Jesus' credentials as the Son of the living God and initiator of God's kingdom? Who can question the importance of miracles in the spread of the gospel in the founding of the church in the book of Acts?

We cannot be sure how much of this pattern God now wants us to use, but we cannot set aside arbitrarily the possibility that He again is working in this way. Indeed, the rapid growth of the Pentecostal churches in North America and overseas, especially Latin America, would seem to indicate this. So would the growth of the charismatic movement among Roman Catholics and the ways in which mainline denominations are being strengthened spiritually through this fresh demonstration of the Spirit's presence.

From Theory to Practice

Applying the theory is as much a part of sound education as deriving the theory. We have learned that spiritual growth comes not only by talking about it, but by engaging in spiritual exercises like prayer, devotional reading, group sharing, personal counseling and public worship.

We have learned also that students need specific help in discovering their spiritual gifts. What has God made them good at? What special equipment or service has the Spirit bestowed on them? Teaching, administration, evangelism, hospitality—these are just a few of the gifts that are listed in Romans 12, Ephesians 4 and 1 Peter 4. Almost all evangelical believers agree that every Christian has at least one gift from these lists and must be encouraged to identify that gift and put it to work in the church.

But what about the gifts listed in 1 Corinthians 12? Do not Christians also need help in seeking them and putting them to work? One role that the signs, wonders and church growth course has played in the lives of our students has been to make them aware of what God may be gifting them to do in powerful service for Him.

The Seminary's Role

None of what is said in this report should be heard as depicting life at Fuller as one huge camp meeting. There were hundreds of students who scarcely knew that Wimber and Wagner were offering the course under discussion.

Our mission in the course was not to inculcate these practices into our student body. It was to provide opportunity for those who wanted the course to see what God had in it for them.

Our role was to provide the opening. God's responsibility was to determine how to use it. The long-term results are up to Him.

DAVID ALLAN HUBBARD *has been president of Fuller Theological Seminary since 1963. He is the author of 31 books, one of the latest being* Unwrap Your Spiritual Gifts.

DISCUSSION QUESTIONS

1. What were some of the risks given in respect to changing the practices and beliefs within the church, especially with signs and wonders? Using the scriptures here, discuss how we can deal with and counter such risks: Prov. 15:32,33; Prov. 24:3,4; Rom. 12:3-21; Eph. 4:1-3; 1 Pet. 4:7-10.
2. What were some of the risks involved in *resisting* change?

Consider these risks in light of the following scriptures: Prov. 13:10; Luke 18:7-14; Rom. 14:10-12; Eph. 4:17-24; Col. 3:12-17.

3. What is the main idea that David Hubbard seems to be advocating?

4. Do you know which of the gifts listed in Rom. 12, Eph. 4, 1 Pet. 4 and 1 Cor. 12 you have? How can your gift be used to its best advantage within the church?

5. Is it possible to accept the existence of such gifts as teaching, preaching and hospitality, but deny the existence of such "wondrous" gifts as healing, tongues and discernment?

APPLICATION

Discuss the possibility within your group of holding a "Spiritual Gifts Workshop." Would this be advantageous for your church? Do you know someone to lead such a session, and how would it be done? One possible study is the *Spiritual Gifts Workshop and Teacher's Guide*, which C. Peter Wagner has developed to go along with his best-selling book *Your Spiritual Gifts Can Help Your Church Grow*. You may also want to consider using Wagner's *Spiritual Gifts Workshop* video cassettes, which will bring your group directly under his teaching for a complete five-to-six-hour spiritual gifts discovery seminar. All these resources are available from The Charles E. Fuller Institute, Box 91990, Pasadena, CA 91109, or call 1-818-449-0425, or outside California 1-800-C.FULLER.

If no leader is available, go back to the scriptures in Question 4. Write down any questions or concerns you may have about gifts, and discuss them in small groups of two-to-four people. Consider the questions raised prayerfully, maintaining an attitude of encouragement and love. Remember, the goal is not to judge, but to understand.

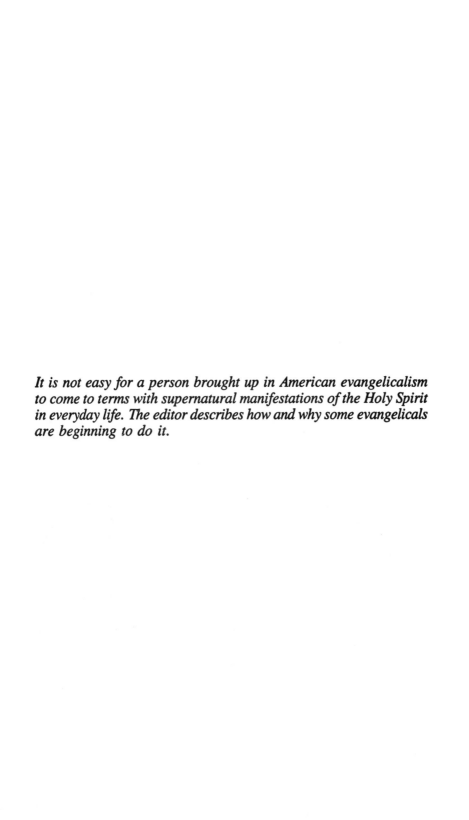

It is not easy for a person brought up in American evangelicalism to come to terms with supernatural manifestations of the Holy Spirit in everyday life. The editor describes how and why some evangelicals are beginning to do it.

2

Signs and Wonders: What Difference Do They Make?

by C. Peter Wagner

One day recently a truly godly man who has been a missionary to American Indians for his entire career told me this story.

A creek that ran through the Indian village where he lived with his family was swollen almost to flood stage. In the midst of the storm an Indian family suddenly realized that their four-year-old child, Ernie, had disappeared. Desperately they began a search, but darkness fell and so did their hopes. In the dim light of the next day, they and their friends scoured the fields, woods and creek banks without success.

Ernie's grandmother was a neighbor of my missionary friend. When all hope of finding the child was dashed, she went to the missionary's home. She had hardly even acknowledged the presence of the missionary and his family, but now she was desperate, ready to try anything.

Can God Find Ernie?

"My grandson is lost in the storm. Will you pray to your God and ask him to bring Ernie back to us?" the grandmother pled.

Surprised at suddenly being recognized as a source of help, the missionary's wife replied, "Of course." She prayed a simple prayer with the grandmother, and asked God to keep Ernie safe wherever he was and bring him back soon.

The Indian grandmother had hardly returned to her home when an uncle came running up the hill shouting, "Ernie's found!"

My friend told me his reaction. To him it was a coincidence, pure and simple; Ernie actually had been found before the prayer was offered. There could have been no cause and effect relationship.

But the grandmother interpreted the events otherwise. For months afterward, the missionaries would be stopped on the street by total strangers and asked to pray for a family problem, a sickness, alcoholism or what have you.

"Your God is powerful—I need His power," these Indians would say. The news of Ernie had spread like wildfire. The God of the missionaries now was tremendously appealing to the Indians.

Power With Little Growth

What was the outcome of this tangible, well-publicized display of God's power? Was it a repetition of the large ingatherings of the book of Acts following the "signs and wonders"?

Unfortunately, this power demonstration had little or no effect on the spread of the gospel in that village.

My missionary friend and I asked ourselves why. Was it because he and his wife refused to recognize God's hand in even the "little" things of life? Was it because they failed to acknowledge that God said, "Before you call, I will answer"? I admitted that during my sixteen years as a missionary to Bolivia I did not see the supernatural power of God working through me at all. We compared our backgrounds. We were Bible-believing, born-again, evangelical Christians. We had been graduated from the right colleges and seminaries. We were ordained by the right churches and had joined the right missions. We defended the evangelical doctrines and lived the evangelical life-style.

But no part of this blue chip background had prepared us to deal adequately with a culture where spirit powers were seen to be at work in every area of life, and where the clash between divine and satanic power often was felt. In fact, much of our training had led us to doubt whether God's activity in the signs and wonders of the New Testament had outlived the apostolic age. The inadequacy of this training became clear to my friend sometime after the lost-boy incident when he found himself face to face with demons which he finally succeeded in casting out of an Indian woman.

Today's Challenge

I am not one to lament the past. But I do want to meet the challenges of the present and future with every resource available. Roughly speaking, there are three billion persons in the world who do not profess to be Christians. Add to this many hundreds of millions who profess Christianity but who lack the life-changing experience of the new birth, and the challenge is clear. To bring these people into the kingdom of God is a formidable task, complicated by the fact that the vast majority of them are at a cultural distance from the witness of practicing Christians. They can be reached only by cross-cultural evangelism.

One of today's foremost missiologists is Paul G. Hiebert, a colleague of mine at the Fuller School of World Mission. Hiebert, who has a commanding grasp of the tools of modern social sciences, also has been wrestling with the problem that my missionary friend and I had encountered. What in our background has left us so relatively impotent when it comes to dealing with supernatural power?

Worldview Is a Key

Hiebert concludes that it has much to do with our worldview. In an article published in the January 1982 *Missiology: An International Review*, he argues that our Western worldview has a blind spot which makes it difficult for many Western missionaries to understand, let alone answer, problems related to spirits, ancestors and astrology.

"As a Westerner," Hiebert says, "I was used to presenting Christ on the basis of rational arguments, not by evidences of His power in the lives of people who were sick, possessed and destitute."

Hiebert traces the development of this Western worldview

back to the seventeenth and eighteenth centuries. Secularized science began explaining natural phenomenon without reference to the supernatural. Religion was allowed to deal with cosmic forces, sacred rituals and possible exceptions to the natural order, but it had little to do with the problems of everyday life. And religion was regarded as unscientific. The result: Our Western worldview became highly conditioned with what many Christian leaders today are calling "secular humanism."

Secular humanism is not just "out there." It has infiltrated our churches, Bible schools and seminaries. This creates problems enough when attempting to minister to fellow Westerners. But these problems are multiplied when we Westerners go out as missionaries to the cultures of the Third World.

It may be a startling revelation to some, but the fact is that most of the world's non-Christians cannot understand or relate to our Western worldview.

What does this mean? Hiebert points out that when tribal people speak of fear of evil spirits, many Western missionaries attempt to deny the existence of the spirits rather than claim the power of Christ over them. As a result, "Western Christian missions have been one of the greatest secularizing forces in history."

What missionary—or Christian layperson—has thought of himself or herself as a secularizer?

I for one never did. But as I look back on my own experience, I now see that it was true. Oh, there was some tangible blessing in the work. Souls were saved and churches were planted. But I now suspect that God was able to do only a fraction of what He wanted to do through me. Why? For the same reason that Jesus' followers could not cast the demon out of the boy—because of unbelief.

Seeing the Bible More Clearly

All this is helping me read the Bible with clearer insight. I now see that each of the five classic appearances of the Great Commission in the New Testament has a power promise.

- "All power is given unto me" (Matt. 28:18).
- "These signs shall follow them that believe" (Mark 16:17).

22

- "Tarry in Jerusalem until ye be endued with power from on high" (Luke 24:49).
  - "Receive ye the Holy Ghost" (John 20:22).
  - "Ye shall receive power" (Acts 1:8).

I now find myself raising the question: How can we—at home or abroad—possibly complete the task of world evangelization without the promised power regularly operating through us? I doubt that it can be done.

The book of Acts is no museum piece. It is a dynamic guidebook as to how the gospel of Jesus, accompanied by the power of the Holy Spirit, penetrates new territory. When Jesus sent out His disciples for the first time, He told them not only to preach that the kingdom of God is at hand, but also to heal the sick, cleanse the lepers, raise the dead and cast out demons (Matt. 10:7-8).

An accumulating body of missiological research is indicating that, worldwide, where the gospel is spreading most rapidly it is doing so with signs and wonders following. At the beginning of the decade of the '80s, I felt that God wanted me to concentrate on the relationship of supernatural signs and wonders to church growth during the decade. I am now amazed by what has been going on that I knew little about.

Evangelicals Are Changing

One thing that is surprising me is how open fellow evangelicals are to rethinking their position and opening themselves to new dimensions of God's power. Whenever I say this I need to avoid misunderstanding by making my position clear. I am not advocating that we all become Pentecostals or charismatics. I am a Congregationalist and do not intend to change. My belief is that God desires to work through all His people in powerful ways, leaving our denominational commitments intact.

It is now generally conceded that we are living in the time of the greatest harvest of souls the world has ever seen. Whether this indicates that the second coming of Christ is near, I do not know for sure, but it does seem like it. If it is true that the harvest is here and that signs and wonders constitute one of the dynamics which God is using for reaping that harvest, then God's people, no matter what their theological tradition, should pay attention. And they are.

Many Pentecostals who have become somewhat nominal in their Pentecostal practices are now getting a new lease on life. Many non-Pentecostals are tuning into the "third wave" and seeing God begin to use them in healings and deliverances. Traditional evangelical pastors are attending signs and wonders seminars led by John Wimber and others. Seminaries across the nation are taking seriously the supernatural power of the Holy Spirit and introducing courses into their curricula which they would not have considered five or ten years ago. This book is the story of one of them, Fuller Theological Seminary in Pasadena, California.

What are they discovering? That supernatural signs and wonders, while not God's only methodology for reaping the harvest, do make a difference.

DISCUSSION QUESTIONS

1. How do you view reports of demon possession, spiritual healings or intercessory prayer? Do you feel prepared to deal with such occurrences?
2. What is meant by "worldview"? What is your worldview, and how does it affect your openness to the issue of signs and wonders?
3. How do you react to the statement: "As a result, Western Christian missions have been one of the greatest secularizing forces in history"? What basis do you have for agreeing or disagreeing with this idea?
4. Can we, through our unbelief, limit God's ability to work through us? (Matt. 13:58; Matt. 17:14-20)
5. What is your reaction to Christ's command in Matt. 10:7-8? Can you mention any cases of this type of ministry today?
6. Discuss the following scriptures and what they have to say to us today: Mark 16:15-20; Acts 1:8; Acts 2:41-47;

Signs and Wonders: What Difference Do They Make?

Acts 4:23-31; Acts 14:1-3; Rom. 15:18-19; 2 Cor. 12:12; Heb. 2:1-4.

APPLICATION

1. On a piece of paper, make two columns. In the first column, list the things that seem to support the idea of signs and wonders as a valid part of today's Christianity. In the second column, list any questions, hesitancies, doubts or fears that you may have in this area. Separate into small groups and share what you have listed. (Make sure each person has time to speak.)
2. As a group, look up 1 John 4:1-6 and 1 Thess. 5:19-22. Discuss the importance of these scriptures as you seek God's leading in your personal lives.
3. Have each person in your group read C. Peter Wagner's exciting book, *Spiritual Power and Church Growth* (Creation House). It will broaden your horizons as to what God is doing in the world today.

Can signs and wonders help churches grow? Much can be learned from Vineyard Christian Fellowship of Anaheim, California, and no one could tell the story better than its founding pastor.

3

Zip to 3,000
In Five Years

by John Wimber

It was happening again! Sunday after Sunday I had been teaching from the book of Luke. Now, for almost twenty weeks, I had been teaching about God's healing power. Often God would prompt me to have an altar call so those who needed prayer could come forward.

Always I obeyed. Yet no one was healed!

Week after week I watched as dear people with high hopes—who believed what I told them from the Bible—came forward for prayer. Every week we prayed. But no one got well. In fact, some of those who prayed for the sick became ill. We were powerless. I was always so hopeful that God would honor what His Word said. Yet each week was the same. Nothing happened.

Now I was looking in the faces of fifty people who had come forward to receive prayer for healing. Hurting people who wanted our help and the Savior's healing touch that I had promised them from the Scriptures. Again I followed them into our prayer room, accompanied by the men and women who were standing faithfully with me in this discouraging enterprise.

We laid our hands on each of them and prayed, asking God to heal their bodies. Hopefully. Expectantly. With all the faith we had, we prayed for them.

But nothing happened. Each left our prayer room still sick. I was filled with despair. I was embarrassed, powerless and helpless to do any more than I had done. I couldn't go on!

I threw myself to the floor and wept. I cried and prayed until there was no strength left in me. I had done all I knew to do. I was mad at God. I was confused. How could I explain what was happening? Wasn't our faith good enough? When I finally lifted my face off the floor, I saw several men who had been crying with me. It was a terrible Sunday!

That was only four years ago!

Building an Army

With all my heart I believed healing is at the core of what Jesus came to accomplish. But when we set our minds to follow Him in this area, we had no idea how painful the learning process would be. It was almost as if we had to prove our faith by persevering in the face of repeated failure.

But I knew it was that kind of evidential Christian faith I wanted. I wanted a Christian faith that I could see. One that worked. If that were not available to me, I would have had difficulty continuing in the ministry.

It was only after a year of painful praying for the sick that we finally saw people healed. But once it began to happen, it happened regularly.

Today, in 1982, we see fifty to 100 people a week healed in our services. Many more are healed as we pray for them in hospitals, on the streets and in homes. The blind are seeing. The lame are walking. The deaf are hearing. Cancers are disappearing.

As a pastor, the most exciting part is that these things are occurring primarily through the ministry of my people.

When I started the church five years ago, I knew that I did not want to build an audience. I wanted to build an army. As a pastor, I began to recognize the high priority of equipping the saints. Today in our church of over 3,000, I would estimate that as many as twenty percent regularly see someone healed through their prayers.

How did it happen?

Fuller Changed Me

After serving five years as a co-pastor in a rapidly growing Friends church in Southern California, I was invited by Fuller Seminary professor Peter Wagner to work with the Fuller Evangelistic Association. Wagner was teaching in the School of World Mission at the seminary and giving part-time leadership to the emerging church growth department at the evangelistic association. I took over the leadership of what ultimately became the Charles E. Fuller Institute for Evangelism and Church Growth.

For the next four years I worked with twenty-seven denominations, nine para-church organizations and hundreds of local churches. I traveled across America speaking to thousands of pastors and serving as a church growth consultant.

My time with the Fuller Evangelistic Association was a tremendous educational experience. The extensive exposure to church life I experienced during my term opened my eyes to the fact that God was bigger than I had ever before realized. But I no longer was personally involved in reaching the lost, and that bothered me. God began to stir up in me a desire to return to the pastorate.

My experiences at the evangelistic association and at the seminary had changed me. I went back into the pastoral ministry a different person. What had happened?

Fuller Seminary professor Paul Hiebert had introduced me to the crucial issue of "worldview." His paper in the January 1982 *Missiology* on the "excluded middle" challenged me again to understand more clearly the powerful implications of our own worldviews.

Meanwhile, professor Charles Kraft stimulated me to apply these principles of worldview to the communication process and to my theology in general.

From Peter Wagner I learned to love the whole church and became open to seeing what the Holy Spirit was doing around the world.

Then Donald McGavran, known worldwide for his enormous contribution to the subject of church growth, inspired in me a fierce pragmatism. I knew after exposure to him that I would never again be satisfied with church life as I had known it.

The Wounded Flock

Not only was I a different person, I had a different sense of mission. I remember God leading me to Ezekiel 34:4: "Those who are sickly you have not strengthened, the diseased you have not healed, the broken you have not bound up, the scattered you have not brought back, nor have you sought for the lost; but with force and severity you have dominated them."

I was a wayward shepherd returning to a wounded flock. But I was not going back to do business as usual. God was sending me back to do what Jesus had done. It was at that time that God underscored Jesus' mission in the world by reminding me of Luke 4:17-18: "The Spirit of the Lord is upon me, because He has anointed me to preach the gospel to the poor. He has sent me to proclaim release to the captives, and recovery of sight to the blind, to set free those who are downtrodden, to proclaim the favorable year of the Lord."

Desiring to have a church as I wanted is one thing; having it is something else.

Many agonizing disappointments came along the way. But my people and I kept hungering for more of what we knew God could do to us and through us. We did not want to be satisfied. We kept wanting more! God took us—a worn-out bunch of Pharisees—and turned us into a band of followers who no longer are governed by our fears of fanaticism or what people will say about us.

Worship and Healing

God took us as He found us—broken-bodied refugees from various religious systems—and began to shape us into a believing group of followers who hungered after Him. Along the way God showed me that it was His church and He didn't need *me* to build it!

How did He start? What things has God taught us over these past five years? As I see it, there have been several developmental phases. Each phase has left its mark on us as a fellowship.

One of the first things God taught us was the value of worship.

In those early days, worship became vital to us. It was all we could do. We were so weak and sick ourselves we had nothing to offer Him except our praise. As we worshipped God, we began to get well.

Also as time passed, we saw a community mentality beginning to emerge.

We began to have one heart and one mind. Out of this, the essential nature of Christian fellowship became a reality in our midst. We really cared for one another. Small groups sprang up with very little organization. They happened then and continue to happen today because we need them.

Along the way as we got healthier, we began again to pray for the sick.

This has been a long and painful process. But because we were in it together as a body, we did not give up. Healing was not just my idea. It was something many saw as a part of our mission as a church. Today it is a common practice of our church life to see the sick healed.

When God Came

Techniques are not enough. There must be power from on high. About three years ago, God visited us in power. Until then, we had experienced the presence of God, but in May 1979, we began to experience His power. Today, our large and small gatherings are characterized by things that I had known about only from history books. Quaking, shaking, falling under the power of God and the public exercise of spiritual gifts such as words of knowledge and prophecy are commonplace. When this kind of thing first occurred, I was deeply troubled until I became convinced from the Scriptures and history that it was from the Lord.

I remember clearly the first evening God visited us powerfully.

I stayed up all night searching the Scriptures and my various histories of revivals for assurance that it was from the Lord. Reviewing the Scriptures and historical accounts helped somewhat, but I still had some questions. The fact was that over the next two months we baptized 700 new converts as a result of this mighty empowering work of the Holy Spirit.

Today we unapologetically honor the Holy Spirit and what He is doing in our midst. We are moving ahead in His power. We also are learning to live with what we don't understand.

Caring for the Poor

Recently God led us to take a new step in our development: to care for the poor in earnest.

Several major efforts have been organized to assist those who are less fortunate. The past two summers we devoted thousands of hours and significant financial resources to refurbishing the homes of needy families in Orange County. Last Easter we gave our entire offering to the Orange County Rescue Mission to feed, clothe and counsel the poor.

It is our intention to make care for the poor a vital part of our on-going ministry.

Worship, fellowship, healing, power and compassion are words that describe the aspects of our church.

But what we do occurs in an environment, a setting that is itself as important as the things we do. To understand the church that has given birth to a signs-and-wonders ministry, it is important to understand something about this environment which is more caught than taught.

A Baby Boom Church

Today in the America of 1982, 78 million people are packed between the baby boom ages of 17 and 35. An additional 54 million are under the age of 17. These 132 million people will determine the future of the American church in the '80s and '90s.

When our church began, the average age was about 19. Today it is up to about 21. We are a young church.

For the most part, the organized church in America is not relating to the younger generation.

The pre-war generation is beginning to pass from the evangelical church scene without replacing itself. Few churches are effectively reaching the young—those who do not feel comfortable with the life-style, music or jargon of establishment Christianity. We are reaching them. As a young church, we experience all of the opportunities and problems which accompany youth. Our young 18- to 25-year-old attenders are providing the spiritual dynamic which enables us to reach out to a young culture and relate the gospel to them.

A Contemporary Church

Because we are young, we are current. We speak the language of these people. Our sermons and songs are familiar and acceptable. We find ourselves communicating eternal truths in a contemporary style. We recognize we must answer the questions people actually are asking.

Jim Wallis, editor of *Sojourners*, said in a recent *Newsweek* article, "What evangelicals need most is biblical living, not biblical talking."

I agree. We seek to deal with today's issues in a practical, biblical manner—a manner that will make a difference in the way people actually live.

A "Second Marriage" Church

Many people who find their way into our services have had some kind of religious background. This is not unusual. Although the numbers are declining, most people in America have had some kind of religious heritage or exposure.

George Gallup, in his studies on American church life, underscores the fact that America is a nation of nominal believers. Although there are more than 100 million church members, only 40-60 million people can be found in church on Sunday morning. He described us well when he said we are a nation of "believers who don't belong."

Many people have chosen to opt out of the religious system because they felt they couldn't live up to the standards the church set for them. Others have been battered and burned by well meaning, but harsh, treatment. Cultural differences have made it difficult for others to relate to the traditional church.

Many of these religious refugees are finding us.

A Church That Ministers in Power

Today in America there is a tremendous increase in the occult, spiritism and all sorts of demonic activity. In their search for spiritual reality, people are seeking new modes of religious thought. The West is looking to the East for a faith.

We believe that Jesus ministered in power to the total person. His message was not for the mind alone; it also was for the spirit and body. Jesus preached, taught *and* healed. We believe this kind of balanced ministry is needed today if the church is to minister as Jesus intends.

People in our culture need to see that God is more powerful than the life-styles they are serving. We are discovering that scripturally defined signs and wonders are playing a major role in getting the gospel message out to a nation that needs help and spiritual direction.

But our ministry style does not flow directly from the pre-war models of the faith healers. We are a body ministry.

Men and women alike have the power and authority to pray for the sick and to minister in all the spiritual gifts. Some are more adept than others, but no one is exempt. The ministry is for everyone.

In our services we expect the Lord both to heal and to reveal His will through prophetic words. This occurs in a warm, rational and orderly environment. Visitors often remark, "This is not what I have seen in the past."

At times, people are led quietly from the larger meeting into our prayer room because they are experiencing a manifestation of God's power such as shaking or weeping. Indeed, our church ministers in the power of the Holy Spirit, and God seems pleased with our trust in Him.

A Church With a Mission

We desire to reach out to people who have not been reached by traditional approaches to the Christian faith. And our mission is to equip believers to do the work of the ministry.

First we intend to reach the people around us, right here in Orange County.

After that, we want to establish outposts around the earth which will do the same. We have already helped to establish six new churches in the United States and abroad. Many more are needed. More are on the way. We expect, together with like-minded groups, to establish fifty new fellowships over the next year. Since these will be born out of a common environment, they will share a common style and will be conforming to the preaching, teaching and healing ministry of Jesus.

A Church With a Sense of Expectancy

We believe that God is at work in the world today as never before. We fully expect Him to intervene in world affairs and in our lives. Attenders of our church are not afraid to encourage one another to develop an emotional relationship with God in addition to the intellectual relationship so strongly encouraged by today's evangelicals.

We encourage each other to "expect God to do more than you have ever believed Him to do or have ever seen Him do." Our spiritual muscles are expanding. We are willing to interpret and understand our experiences as we go.

What the future holds for us and other churches in the next decade is open to much speculation. Our perception is that a tremendous spiritual hunger exists in America and around the world. We fully expect that God will allow the life-changing message of the gospel to be presented throughout every nation on earth. We look forward to being a part of this great adventure.

JOHN WIMBER *is the founding pastor of the Vineyard Christian Fellowship of Anaheim, California, and president of Vineyard Ministries International. He taught the course, MC510, Signs, Wonders and Church Growth, at Fuller Seminary 1982-1985. His books* Power Evangelism *and* Power Healing *are helping thousands of Christians understand what God is doing today.*

DISCUSSION QUESTIONS

1. How do you react when faced with doubts, and what may seem to be spiritual failure? Read the following scriptures. What do they have to say to us in reference to our endurance of trials? (1 Kings 19:4-8; Job 42:1-17; 2 Cor. 11:21-33; James 1:2-7)

2. How do you view the responsibilities of a pastor or church

leader in this connection? (1 Tim. 3:1-7; 1 Pet. 5:1-4)

3. Do you feel that it is your responsibility, either as individuals or as a church group, to fulfill the mission of the Spirit as it is presented in Luke 4:16-19?

4. Are there aspects of your faith that you have had to learn to live with without understanding? How do you feel about this kind of "blind faith"?

5. Discuss each of the six characteristics of Vineyard Christian Fellowship church in respect to your church or group. Use the following questions as you discuss:

1) What age groups are being reached effectively in your church? Are there areas that need improvement? How can this be implemented?

2) What are your church's methods of communication? Are these being used to deal with problems in a practical, biblical manner? If not, what can you do to change this? (2 Tim. 3:14-17)

3) Is the atmosphere of your church or group one of acceptance? How would a "religious refugee" feel if he visited? How should we behave in a case such as this? (Rom. 14:1,3,7,8,10)

4) What is meant by "ministering in power" (2 Tim. 1:6-11)? Does your church have a "body ministry"? How do you feel about this type of ministry?

5) Is there an outreach program in your church? Do you feel it is effective? Why or why not? How does like-mindedness come into play in outreach? (Gal. 5:7-10; Phil. 3:15-16)

6) What is meant by a sense of "expectancy" (Mark 11:24; James 1:5-8)? Do you feel such a sense in your personal relationship with God or in the church? How can you develop this expectant type of faith, and how does it tie in with a ministry of signs and wonders?

APPLICATION

1. Read Ephesians 4:11-16 and discuss what can be done

within your church to "equip the saints." Use 1 Corinthians 14:26 and Ephesians 4:22-32 for guidelines.

2. Develop a practical "game plan" for your church or group in this area. Determine where you should start: workshops, special teaching sessions, discussion groups to determine interest and so forth. If your church has not had a ministry of healing, you may want to identify other churches in your area which do and visit them.

3. Agree together who will do what, and be willing to make a serious commitment of time and energy to ensure an effective and productive time of training and "equipping" of those in your church who are interested.

4. If you would like to follow up on this subject, order John Wimber's audio tapes, "Signs, Wonders and Church Growth," Parts I and II. They are available from Vineyard Ministries International (P.O. Box 65004, Anaheim, CA 92805).

When Fuller Seminary began teaching a course in signs and wonders in 1982, it was moving into uncharted territory. The professor of record tells the story of how it all began.

4

MC510:
Genesis of a Concept

by C. Peter Wagner

Kwang Soon Lee is one of the most highly respected leaders in her Presbyterian church in Korea. An attractive, articulate woman in her thirties, her career was unfolding beautifully. She had been elected to head up the 500,000-member women's movement in her denomination. But she felt she should postpone her acceptance until she finished her Ph.D. at the Fuller Seminary School of World Mission. Her dissertation topic: "The Role of Women in the Christian Movement in Korea." Her world was neat, orderly, predictable.

But while she was studying, Kwang Soon's dream turned into emptiness. Her eyes had been troubling her, so she went to the doctor. The diagnosis: a severe case of glaucoma. There was a high possibility that she would gradually become blind. Kwang Soon turned to God and recommitted her life to Him. While she was willing to accept God's will, she cried out for healing. She believed God wanted to use her—with her eyesight.

As Kwang Soon and others were praying about her disease, she became aware of an extraordinary thing that God was doing at Fuller Seminary during the winter quarter of 1982. From fellow students she began hearing stories of a new class titled MC510, Signs, Wonders and Church Growth. John Wimber, pastor of the Vineyard Christian Fellowship of Anaheim, was teaching most of the classes. Several students had been telling her of remarkable healings and other manifestations of the Holy Spirit—right in the Fuller Seminary classroom! Then her roommate, who was praying with her against the glaucoma, invited Kwang Soon to visit one of the classes.

The Ministry Time

The three hours of class passed swiftly for Kwang Soon for she had never been exposed to anything like this in either Korea or the United States. Her faith rose to new heights. She cautiously wondered if God might answer her prayer that night. At 10:00 p.m. Wimber dismissed the class as usual. Those who wished to remain for the "ministry time" were invited to do so.

Few of the 100 persons left the room. In fact, some visitors who had come only for the ministry session joined the others.

God spoke through several "words of knowledge." These were specific indications that God wanted to heal some who were there.

One student, for example, thought God was telling her that someone had a problem with the right knee. On the other side of the room my teaching assistant, Bruce Bauer, a veteran Seventh-Day Adventist missionary to Japan, stood up. Immediately a cluster of people seated nearby, who had been trained for several weeks to do this, gathered around him, laid on hands and began to pray. Bruce is an athletic person who likes to run. But his right knee, and also his left one to a degree, had been paining him for weeks. While he could get around, he could not run. God miraculously did as He indicated He would that night. As I write this a month later, Bruce is still running full speed with no pain!

There was no such word of knowledge for Kwang Soon Lee. But then Wimber invited those who needed healing to stand and share their problems with those around them.

Kwang Soon was on her feet, and a group gathered to minister to her. This was not a fast-moving healing line. The group prayed with her for possibly a half hour. As they did they began to believe that God was doing the healing.

However, the symptoms of glaucoma are different from those of painful knees. There was no way of knowing for sure what happened that night. But Kwang Soon left rejoicing.

Since then she has been examined by two doctors. The first said, "The pressure is much better. Come back in two months." She went to a second doctor twice, just to make sure. Her eye pressure was normal.

The How and the Why

Why did the Fuller School of World Mission begin teaching a course in signs, wonders and church growth?

John Wimber and I have been close friends since 1975. At that time he was a Quaker pastor in a growing church in Orange County. We met when he enrolled for my Church Growth I course in the Fuller doctor of ministry program. At that time I was also executive director of the Fuller Evangelistic Association. God had been speaking to me about starting a church growth department there so that some of the church growth theories which were being worked out by Donald McGavran, me and others in the seminary could be translated into practical resources for people in the local churches. I recognized Wimber's gifts and invited him to pioneer the department. He left his pastorate and teamed up with me. God blessed the ministry, and it is now under the direction of Carl George with the name The Charles E. Fuller Institute of Evangelism and Church Growth.

After Wimber had established the Fuller Institute, God called him to pastor the budding Vineyard Christian Fellowship of Yorba Linda. The original Bible study actually had been started by his wife, Carol, in their living room. That group of about seventeen now has grown in five years to about 3,000. Wimber tells the story of how this happened in another chapter in this book. As he explains, fairly early in the process God began doing some remarkable things in the ministry of healing in the new church.

By that time Wimber had become an adjunct professor in our School of World Mission and was doing some teaching with me in my doctor of ministry course called Church Growth II. One day he suggested to me that he take a class session on signs, wonders and church growth.

This was a new thought to me, but God had been preparing me for my response.

That preparation was not automatic. Nothing from my early Christian background would have predisposed me to be open to such a suggestion. I had served for sixteen years under two missions which were members of the Interdenominational Foreign Missions Association. One of the written policies of this association is "Each mission will have clearly stated articles of faith consistent with the IFMA Confession of Faith, and will maintain a non-charismatic orientation."

I had taken my M.Div. at Fuller Seminary in the '50s and my Th.M. at Princeton Seminary in the '60s. Nothing I can recall in those educational experiences would have opened my mind to believing that God could and does work in miraculous ways in this day and age. I was a dispensationalist who carried a Scofield Bible and could construct all the charts from memory. I recall very clearly that when a faith healer came to our city of Cochabamba, Bolivia, I warned our Bolivian believers not to go to the meetings and wrote an article for a national evangelical magazine refuting his claims.

How My Mind Changed

Then God began to work in me. Not by some flash of lightning that changed me in ten minutes, but gradually over the last five years of my missionary career. As I think back I believe that a couple of events in particular contributed to opening a new dimension of the work of God to me.

The first event was a meeting held in Cochabamba by E. Stanley Jones. While we were warned that we shouldn't go to hear him because he was purported to be a liberal, my wife and I surreptitiously attended and sat toward the back of the room.

The meeting turned out to be an old-fashioned healing service. I myself happened to be suffering from an open, festering cyst in my neck which my surgeon had scheduled for a second surgery a week from then. I was too embarrassed to go forward when Jones gave the invitation because I wasn't supposed to be there. But later, when he invited those of us still in our seats to trust God for healing, I did. When I got home I took off the bandage and went to bed. The next morning the running sore had dried up and hasn't bothered me since. The process had begun.

Pentecostals in Chile

The second event was a series of visits to Chile where I came into close contact with the Chilean Pentecostals.

While I had been one of the chief adversaries of the Pentecostals in Bolivia, somehow God opened my heart and mind to accept at face value what was happening in Chile. By that time I had studied church growth under Donald McGavran and, if nothing else, was attracted by the phenomenal growth of the Chilean Pentecostal churches. There I witnessed healings, speaking in tongues, concert prayers, baptisms in the Spirit, dancing in the Spirit, prophecies, visions—just as if they were a normal part of the twentieth-century Christian experience.

So fascinated did I become that I wrote a book now called *Spiritual Power and Church Growth* (Creation House) describing what God is doing in Latin American Pentecostalism. I began to love Pentecostals and still do.

While these events have had a lasting effect on me, I have not detected any leading of God to become either a Pentecostal or a charismatic. I belong to Lake Avenue Congregational Church in Pasadena, California, and love my church dearly. I have no intention of ever joining another church. I'm just a straightline evangelical.

But by the time John Wimber asked me about teaching on signs and wonders, I was ready. I gave him the green light, and he taught the first class in the summer session of 1981.

It went well. He had done some excellent research. I thought it was something new and important that we should probe in the church growth field. Then he shared some further ideas for teaching.

McGavran's Imprimatur

Meanwhile I had discovered God was doing something else. Donald McGavran is the world-renowned founder of the church growth movement and my own mentor. For two or three years, I learned, he had been giving a lecture on divine healing and church growth in his advanced church growth course here in the Fuller School of World Mission. This, for me, was like a papal *imprimatur*. If it was all right for Donald McGavran, it was all right for me.

The further idea that John Wimber had was to teach a whole seminary course on signs, wonders and church growth. He had been doing a substantial amount of research on the matter, and he had a good team of assistants to do more. He also had the experience of seeing how the miraculous works of God were actually relating to the growth of his own church, and he had learned how to teach others to pray for the sick with considerable power.

For me the plot was thickening. I could decide on my own to let Wimber teach a class on signs and wonders in my Church Growth II course, but a new course in the curriculum would be a matter for faculty decision. I told him I would bring it up and see how the faculty would respond.

The Reaction of the Faculty

The members of the Fuller School of World Mission faculty are a very close-knit team led by Paul Pierson, the dean. We know each other well. We love each other. We support each other in prayer, and we encourage each other in our careers. But we had never talked about this particular dimension of ministry. We come from diverse backgrounds: United Presbyterian, Mennonite, Brethren, United Methodist, Reformed Presbyterian, Congregational, Bible Church. We have served in different parts of the world: Brazil, India, Nigeria, Bolivia, China, Jamaica, Portugal, Singapore. This makes it all the more remarkable that the faculty was unanimous in voting in favor of the proposed course.

As we shared, we found that most of us had similar experiences during our years on the mission field. We were aware of demons and supernatural powers, but our own ministry had never really touched them. In theory we knew and believed that God was the Lord of the principalities and powers. We taught that the spirit world was real. We had even theorized about the efficacy of the power encountered in missiological situations.

Dean Gilliland, professor of contextualization of theology, shared a typical experience in his new book, *Pauline Theology and Mission Practice* (Baker).

The Sad Story of Nuhu

A United Methodist, Gilliland was president of the Theological College of Northern Nigeria at the time. One of his students was a Nigerian pastor named Nuhu. Nuhu had become convinced that his wife was demonized and went to the missionaries for help.

Gilliland says, "I knew the spirit world was real and taught it. I knew also that the Holy Spirit was more powerful. But I felt as if I was teaching with one hand tied behind my back."

Moreover, Gilliland admits, he did not know how to release God's power to deal with demons. So Nuhu did the only thing he could think of. He went to a pagan exorcist! There he saw his wife covered with a blanket while two animistic priests walked around her chanting magic formulas and waving banana leaves. Gilliland continues, "It was sad to realize that there was a believer whose desperation had brought him to trust again in 'those weak and pitiful ruling spirits' " (Gal. 4:9).

The specifics of the story were Gilliland's. But in general he told the story of every one of us sitting in that faculty meeting.

A Theory of Power

Charles Kraft, professor of intercultural communication, said, "We desperately need to develop a theology of power in our school. In this day and age we no longer can maintain our integrity as a School of World Mission and send out people to minister in the Third World without first training them how to pray for the sick." Kraft, along with his wife, Marguerite, who is a professor at Biola University, attended every one of the subsequent Monday night sessions.

While the missions faculty is enthusiastic over the emphasis on the supernatural, we do not want to be naive. Substantial exegetical and empirical studies need to be made in the subject of supernatural activity. Satan and his forces have considerable power as Moses learned from Pharaoh's magicians. Hindus and Muslims speak in tongues. Sorcerers perform miracles. Psychic surgery is uncanny. Faith healings and demon exorcisms happen in other religious systems.

A great deal of spiritual discernment is needed at this point. The Christian faith must not be permitted to degenerate into a pious sort of magic.

Looking to the Future

In 1980, God gave me several research goals for the decade. One was to investigate the relationship of signs and wonders to the growth of the church. When the faculty asked me to assist John Wimber in setting up the course, I shared this interest with him. My personal goal is not to research signs and wonders as ends in themselves, although they are wonderful workings of God. I feel led to discover why sometimes these signs and wonders are accompanied by the growth of churches and sometimes they are not.

This has been a neglected dimension in our church growth research and writing. My friend Herbert Kane, missions professor emeritus at Trinity Evangelical Divinity School, brought this to my attention. In his book *The Christian World Mission Today and Tomorrow*, Kane includes a very supportive chapter on the church growth movement. He judges it to be "the most dynamic movement in mission circles in recent years." But his concluding paragraph asserts, "The proponents of church growth, with few exceptions, have emphasized the human factors and all but overlooked the divine factor."

I take Kane seriously. While we here at Fuller Seminary believe we have maintained a balanced position, and references to the divine factor abound in the works of Donald McGavran, Arthur Glasser, Paul Hiebert and others, Kane makes it clear that all of our friends do not see it that way. Therefore, it is quite important to me that we stress more than ever the sovereign, supernatural, miraculous working of God in the growth of the church worldwide.

The new research project is coming along well. I have several students working on aspects of it. Opal Reddin, a professor in Central Bible College, Springfield, Missouri, is combing the Assemblies of God libraries and archives for information. Christiaan De Wet, a South African from the Apostolic Faith Mission Church, has completed a master's thesis on the subject and has contributed a chapter to this book. Two Koreans are helping: Lee Jae-Bum is researching the Pentecostal movement in Korea, and Lee Yo-Han is working on the famous prayer mountain movement there. Two missionaries, Terrie Lillie and Dennis Brown, are cataloging and documenting case studies of power encounters throughout Christian history.

Yugoslavia and China

Two extremely important projects have emerged directly from the class. Vlasta Kuzmic, whose husband Peter is a seminary professor in Yugoslavia, took the course. She was so impressed that she received a burden for helping her own people become aware of this kind of ministry. So she translated one of the textbooks, *Healing: Reflections on the Gospel* by George Martin, into Serbian and Croatian.

David Wang, general director of Asian Outreach in Hong Kong, also was taking the course. Through his frequent visits to mainland China, he knew that one of the most significant factors stimulating the growth of Christianity from one million in 1950 to more than 30 million in 1982 was a widespread, spontaneous outbreak of supernatural signs and wonders in every province of China. The house church movement has witnessed the miraculous work of God for many years. The gospel is spreading with signs following as it did in the book of Acts.

But this is not without opposition. The Three Self Church leaders do not look favorably on this kind of growth, and several public statements have been made in an attempt to stop it. One of them, recently published in Jonathan Chao's *China Prayer Letter* (April 1982), is found in a list of "Ten Don'ts" issued for Christians to observe in Central China. "Don't" number 6 says, "pray for the sick or exorcise the demons."

Knowing this, David Wang also has translated George

Martin's book into both the traditional and modern Chinese scripts. He asked prayer in the class for funds to publish an initial edition for mainland China. The very same week John Wimber's church, Vineyard Christian Fellowship, took up a special offering and gave David the $4,000 he needed for the special edition.

Where will all this lead us? I am not yet aware of all that God has in store for us. But I have felt for some time that the decade of the 1980s will see more explosive church growth worldwide than any other decade in history. And the best indications are that it already has begun. An increasing number of missiologists are beginning to believe and teach that the great future breakthrough to the Buddhists, Hindus and Muslims will be accompanied with signs and wonders in the New Testament style. And if this is what God desires to do, we in the Fuller School of World Mission do not want to be mere spectators—we want to be participants.

DISCUSSION QUESTIONS

1. What does the term "charismatic" mean to you? Does it usually carry a negative or positive connotation? Would you consider everyone who believes in signs and wonders for today to be a "charismatic" believer?
2. Do you believe that signs and wonders and how they apply to church growth is a valid subject for a seminary to be teaching? If you had been on the faculty of Fuller, how would you have reacted to the question of this course being offered? Why?
3. Consider Ephesians 6:10-18. How does this apply to those involved in ministry—preachers, missionaries, counselors and so on—and their abilities to deal with things on a "supernatural level"? Are the spiritual gifts a part of the "full armor of God"?
4. What do you believe would qualify as "theology of power"? How can we avail ourselves of such a theology or power? (Matt. 9:8; 10:1; Luke 24:49)

5. Read Luke 10:17-20 and discuss its implications. Where did Jesus place the priority?
6. Discuss the importance of spiritual discernment. Where does this type of discernment come from?

APPLICATION

Are you willing to participate in the things that God is doing in many churches today? If your answer is yes, consider the following situation and discuss what your response should be.

A group of people in your church held a healing service. The elders and pastor were unaware of this, and when they discovered it were furious. "You're playing with things that shouldn't be done!" they tell the people. Then they forbid such a thing ever taking place in the church again. Those involved are crushed and confused, sure that God had moved them to involve themselves in a healing ministry. "What should we do?" one of them asks you. (Be sure to base whatever you say on Scripture.)

A large amount of research is now being done at Fuller with the view of understanding the miraculous work of God more clearly and applying it to everyday life. A Fuller student, who is a pastor in South Africa, takes us back to scriptural foundations.

5

Biblical Basis
Of Signs and Wonders
by Christiaan de Wet

There is a sound theological basis for assuming that signs and wonders still are occurring today. That hypothesis can be confirmed by reviewing the biblical concept of the kingdom of God.

Although the phrase "kingdom of God" does not appear in the Old Testament, many scholars agree that the idea can be recognized clearly in the rule of God over the events of history in general and over the nation of Israel in particular.

Jesus' Kingdom Ministry

Early in the New Testament, Matthew reports the message of John the Baptist in the wilderness of Judea: "Repent, for the kingdom of heaven is at hand" (Matt. 3:2). After the baptism of Jesus and His temptation in the wilderness, He went to Capernaum and began His three years of public ministry. Matthew says, "From that time Jesus began to preach, saying, Repent, for the kingdom of heaven is at hand" (Matt. 4:17). Not only did He preach, but He performed all kinds of signs and wonders to confirm His ministry. The blind were healed, the deaf could hear, the dumb could talk, the lame could walk, demons were cast out, and even the dead were raised.

Healing was such a normal part of His ministry that biblical writers could say, "And He went about all Galilee, teaching in their synagogues and preaching the gospel of the kingdom

51

and healing every disease and every infirmity among the people'' (Matt. 4:23).

"Thy kingdom come" was part of the prayer Jesus gave His disciples as an example (Matt. 6:10). When Jesus preached on the kingdom, He explained it in a series of parables, likening it to a sower, a grain of mustard seed, leaven, a hidden treasure, a pearl of great price, a dragnet and a householder (Matt. 13). Jesus stunned the crowds with signs and wonders and startled them with His messages.

He also gave authority to His disciples over unclean spirits, telling them to cast out and to heal every disease and every infirmity, charging them to preach, "The kingdom of heaven is at hand" (Matt. 10:7). They also had to "heal the sick, raise the dead, cleanse the lepers, cast out demons" (Matt. 10:8). Later on, Jesus appointed seventy others and instructed them: "Whenever you enter a town and they receive you, eat what is set before you; heal the sick in it and say to them, 'The kingdom of God has come near to you' '' (Luke 10:8-9).

After the Resurrection

Not only was the kingdom a prominent theme before the resurrection, but ample evidence exists in Scripture that it was a very important theme thereafter. In Acts 1:3 we read that during the forty days between the time Jesus was raised from the dead and His ascension, He spoke to His apostles about "the kingdom of God."

When Philip evangelized Samaria, he "preached the good news about the kingdom of God" (Acts 8:12). In Ephesus, Paul "spoke boldly, arguing and pleading about the kingdom of God" (Acts 19:8). The last thing that we know about Paul in Rome was that he was "preaching the kingdom of God and teaching about the Lord Jesus Christ quite openly and unhindered" (Acts 28:31). Paul, Peter, James and the author of Hebrews all mention the kingdom in their epistles.

The Greek word *basileia* (kingdom) can mean both the geographical area over which a king reigns and the exercise of kingly sovereignty, but it is in the latter sense that the word is used in the New Testament teaching on the kingdom of God.

When the Pharisees accused Jesus of casting out demons by the power of Beelzebub, He made this significant statement about the kingdom: "But if it is by the Spirit of God that I cast out demons, then the kingdom of God has come upon you" (Matt. 12:28).

Ladd and Ridderbos

George Eldon Ladd, one of the world's best-known authorities on the subject of the kingdom, reacts to this verse of Scripture: "What means the announcement that the kingdom of God has come? It is this: that God is now acting among men to deliver them from bondage to Satan...The exorcism of demons is proof that the kingdom of God has come among men and is at work among them. The casting out of demons is itself a work of the kingdom of God."

In his book *The Coming of the Kingdom*, Dutch theologian Herman Ridderbos regards the signs and wonders in the ministry of Jesus as signs of the kingdom. He asserts, "This factual relation between the coming of the kingdom and Jesus' miracles is also brought out not only by the casting out of devils but also by Jesus' other miracles, for they all prove that Satan's power has been broken and that, therefore, the kingdom has come."

In fact, an overwhelming mass of biblical and theological information on the kingdom led me to join the view of many theologians that signs and wonders are signs of the kingdom.

Signs of the Kingdom

A portion of Scripture that needs special attention in this regard is Luke 4:18-19: "The Spirit of the Lord is upon me, because He has anointed me to preach good news to the poor. He has sent me to proclaim release to the captives and recovering of sight to the blind, to set at liberty those who are oppressed, to proclaim the acceptable year of the Lord."

C. Peter Wagner, professor at Fuller Seminary, agrees that spiritualizing the passage does not do justice to it, but that there is a very important literal meaning attached to it. In his *Church Growth and the Whole Gospel*, he expands the list of signs of the kingdom found in Luke by adding others out of Luke

7:21-22 and Mark 16:17-18. Wagner then compounds two general categories of signs of the kingdom:

Category A: Social change or signs applied to a general class of people—1) Preaching good news to the poor; 2) proclaiming release to the captive; 3) liberating the oppressed; 4) instituting the year of Jubilee ("acceptable year of the Lord").

Category B: Personal signs or signs applied to specific individuals—1) Restoring sight to blind people; 2) casting out demons and evil spirits; 3) healing sick people; 4) making lame people walk; 5) cleansing lepers, 6) restoring hearing to deaf people; 7) taking up serpents; 8) raising the dead; 9) speaking in tongues; 10) drinking deadly poison with no ill effects.

Category B signs, Wagner says, are what is generally meant by signs and wonders. "It is what the Bible refers to when it records the prayer of the believers in Jerusalem, 'that *signs* and *wonders* may be done by the name of the holy child Jesus' (Acts 4:30), or the account that Stephen, full of faith and power, 'did great *wonders* and *miracles* among the people' (Acts 6:8), or the testimony of the apostle Paul: 'Truly the signs of an apostle were wrought among you in all patience. In *signs* and *wonders* and *mighty deeds*' (2 Cor. 12:12)....The main function of category B signs is to draw public attention to the power of God in order to open unsaved people's hearts to the message of the gospel.

It also is highly significant that when Jesus sent His disciples out, and also later the seventy, He commissioned them with category B, not category A signs. When Jesus gave the great commission for world evangelization, He said that category B signs would follow the preaching of the disciples (Mark 16:15-18).

Moreover, after Jesus had left the earth, the ministry of His followers continued to be characterized by category B signs: the outpouring of the Holy Spirit at Pentecost (Acts 2:4) and likewise at the house of Cornelius (Acts 10:46); healing and exorcism (Acts 5:16); lame healed (Acts 8:7); Paul bitten by a poisonous snake on Malta with no ill effects (Acts 28:3-5).

Savior Equals Healer

In his book *The New Being*, Paul Tillich, German theologian, sums it up well in saying: "The gospels, certainly, are not responsible for this disappearance of power in the picture of Jesus. They abound in stories of healing; but *we* are responsible—ministers, laymen, theologians—who forgot that 'Savior' means 'healer,' he who makes whole and sane what is broken and insane, in body and mind. The woman who encountered Him was made whole, the demoniac who met Him was liberated from his mental cleavage. Those who are disrupted, split, disintegrated, are healed by Him. And because this is so, because this power has appeared on earth, the kingdom of God has come upon us; this is the answer Jesus gives to the Pharisees when they discuss His power of healing the mentally possessed; this is the answer He gives to the Baptist to overcome his doubts; this is the order He gives to His disciples when He sends them to the towns of Israel. 'And as ye go, preach, saying, the kingdom of God is at hand. Heal the sick, cleanse the lepers, cast out demons.' That is what they shall do and for this He gives them authority and power; for in Him the kingdom of God has appeared and its nature is salvation, healing of that which is ill, making whole what is broken."

Does God Want Us Well?

An important book on this subject is *Salvation and Wholeness*, by rector of St. Mary's, Newick, Sussex, John P. Baker. Baker sees in the teaching of Christ that the kingdom of God comes in three stages: the first coincides with His own person and ministry; the second begins with His exaltation and the outpouring of the Holy Spirit; and the third, the consumatio, ensues upon the *parousia* (the return of Jesus).

For Baker, it is clear that God wants every believer to live healthily until the "number of his days are fulfilled." According to Deuteronomy 34:7, Moses at age 120 had "eyes...not dim nor had his natural strength diminished" and the only reason he died was because God received his spirit when the number of his days was fulfilled.

"One cannot but feel that in general, apart from persecution, war and so on," says Baker, "this is God's intention for those who have consistently let the Spirit of life in Christ Jesus set them free from the law of sin and death at every level of their being: namely that, at the end of a long and full life ('old and full of days') and in good health, they should breathe their last yielding up their spirit to their Maker when He sees that the number of their days (normally 70-80 years now) are fulfilled, for their times are in His hand" (see Gen. 25:8; 35:29; 49:33; Ex. 23:26; Job 42:17; Ps. 31:15; 90:10; 104:29; Eccl. 12:7).

One of the main words for "health" and "healing" in the Old Testament, *arukah*, means literally a "lengthening" or "prolonging" (Is. 58:8; Jer. 8:22). According to Baker, it seems that we have no scriptural warrant for expecting or accepting bad health and illness from middle age onwards, rather we are encouraged to expect good health at least into our 70s as we walk with the Lord. Naturally we must expect all the normal signs of aging, but not necessarily extreme weakness or a lingering and painful illness at the end. Rather it will be an ebbing away of life, speedily at the last, as the Lord either takes the person's spirit to be with Him, or the person yields up his spirit to his Creator in peace of heart and mind.

"In the Bible, forgiveness, healing, eternal life, deliverance from evil and so forth are not separate things or parcels; they are all part and parcel of the one salvation of God in Jesus Christ for His people in the covenant of grace. 'Salvation' and 'healing' are virtually interchangeable terms," Baker says.

The Value of Suffering

Healing as a part of salvation does not rule out the place of suffering in the life of the believer. Suffering, when rightly and meekly borne for Christ's sake, will refine character and strengthen faith, thereby playing its part in producing wholeness (Rom. 5:3-5). The problem with this is that many Christians assert that because of the suffering aspect, disease is to be accepted as part of God's perfect will for them. But this does not necessarily follow. No one will and can doubt that the Lord can and does use disease and disaster to chasten His children in the short term (Ps. 119:67-71), but Peter definitely states that Christians should not regard this as God's perfect will (1 Peter 2-4).

Baker also points out that both the Old and New Testaments show the root causes of disease often are spiritual and emotional, rather than physical. Furthermore, it is Baker's conviction that healing at every level of the person (including the physical) is part of God's provision of salvation during this New Testament age of grace. One of his strongest arguments is that the compound covenant title used in Exodus 15:26, *Yahweh-Rapha* (the Lord [who] heals), is one of seven such titles which are compounded with God's covenant name *Yahweh* in the Old Testament. They all serve as promises to His people as a whole and without discrimination. There is no reason for limiting the extent or validity of one without doing the same for all the others.

Jesus' Commission

When we look at the various commissions of Christ to His disciples and His statement regarding the ministry of the church after His ascension, it becomes clear that Jesus never intended the healing ministry of the church to cease after His death. In the Great Commission of Matthew 28:19, the disciples are told to make disciples of all nations and baptize them, teaching them to observe everything Jesus had commanded them. Plainly in the disciples' minds this "all things" must have included healing and exorcism as in their previous commissions. In the early church many healings took place, and not only through the ministry of the apostles (Acts 8).

In the epistles it is clear that the gospel was preached not only in word, but also in deeds and power through the Holy Spirit (Heb. 2:3-4). Miracles evidently continued in the churches (Gal. 3:1-5). The church members, having been baptized in the Holy Spirit, received gifts of faith, healings, miracle workings and discernment of spirits among others (1 Cor. 12:8). When a believer in the congregation was sick, the elders could be called upon to pray and anoint in the name of Jesus for healing (James 5:14-16).

SIGNS AND WONDERS TODAY

CHRISTIAAN DE WET is a pastor in the Apostolic Faith Mission Church, South Africa's largest Pentecostal denomination. His research on signs and wonders was done during his recent program of studies in the Fuller Seminary School of World Mission.

DISCUSSION QUESTIONS

1. What does the author present as a confirmation of Christ's ministry? Why? How does this serve as confirmation?
2. Do you agree with author Paul Tillich that the responsibility for allowing the miracle-working power of God to operate lies with us (Matt. 13:57-58; Matt. 17:14-21)? If we are indeed responsible, what must we do to meet this responsibility (Acts 7:51; John 15:4-5)?
3. How do you react to John Baker's view on health and our relationship with God? With this view in mind, how do we deal with the realities of sickness and disease...and especially terminal illnesses? How do we reconcile these realities to the fact of the power available to us through God?

APPLICATION

1. Read Psalm 22. What are the emotions expressed in this psalm (vs. 1-21)? How does David counter the negative feelings and despair (vs. 22-25)? What is his final conclusion about the whole situation (vs. 25-31)?
2. Compare David's reactions to your own in a similar situation (that is, when healing or some sign has been prayed for, yet no answer seems to come). Discuss how we can use David's example to deal with such times.

Some say that miracles ceased with the apostolic age. Did they? Some excerpts from the MC510 syllabus indicate that there is evidence of a continued work of the supernatural through history.

6

Miracles Through History
from MC510 Syllabus

In the first 100 years of the church, signs and wonders were a vital and visible activity of the Christian life. In those days it was a byword among Christians: "If you see a brother who is sick and do not heal him, his blood will be on your hands." Healings, signs and wonders were a key part of the proclamation of the gospel.

These phenomena and the zeal which accompanied the early witnesses expanded the church so rapidly that by the end of the first century as many as one-fifth (twenty-four million) of the Roman Empire had been converted. The church was literally taking over the empire. This amazing success helps account for Caesar's persecution of the Christians during that period.

The Fathers and the Reformers

One of the earliest of the church fathers to acknowledge the working of the Holy Spirit in his day was Irenaeus who lived about A.D. 140-203.

He wrote: "We do also hear many brethren in the Church who possess prophetic gifts, and who through the Spirit speak all kinds of languages, and bring to light for the general benefit the hidden things of men, and declare the mysteries of God, whom also the apostle terms 'spiritual.' "

Many other early church fathers both acknowledged and

practiced the gifts of the Holy Spirit. Some of the better known are Justin Martyr, Polycarp, Tertullian, St. Basil, Chrysostom. Even Augustine, who at first thought the gifts of the Spirit of the first century had died out, later in his ministry prayed for the sick and saw healings, exorcised demons and rejoiced at the deliverance of his parishioners.

Later church leaders also accepted signs and wonders as a valid practice. Martin Luther, who had denied the gift of healing for his time, lived to see his friend Melanchthon visibly brought from the point of death through his own prayers. Five years later (the year before he died), when asked what to do for a man who was mentally ill, Luther wrote instructions for a healing service based on the New Testament letter of James, adding, "This is what we do, and what we have been accustomed to do, for a cabinetmaker here was similarly afflicted with madness and we cured him by prayer in Christ's name."

Like the two great saints of the church before him—Augustine and Aquinas—he seems to have learned in his mellower years to value, rather than to disregard, this gift from God.

John Wesley

Both in his *Journal* and in *A Short History of the People Called Methodists*, John Wesley describes a revival meeting in Huntingdonshire in May 1759, conducted by the Rev. Mr. J. Berridge, in which both adults and children fell under the power of the Spirit. "They shrieked, swooned, fell to the floor as if dead, babbled senselessly, cried out in praise of God."

If Wesley had momentary qualms about their authenticity, he quickly put them out of mind. In response to his own sense of danger "to regard extraordinary circumstances too much," Wesley said, "perhaps the danger is, to regard them too little."

Revivals

In the United States, the years between 1800 and 1900 were great years of revival in the frontier areas. Often called the Second Great Awakening, they included a number of special moves of the Holy Spirit, where supernatural and extraordinary gifts of the Spirit were in evidence. Writing on the Cain Ridge meeting of 1801, Aneas McCallister claimed that "like wonders had not been seen except in the Kentucky revival last summer.''

In the summer of 1801, a North Carolina Presbyterian congregation experienced a movement of the Spirit: ''Physical manifestations and speaking in tongues made it like the day of Pentecost and none was careless or indifferent.''

Meanwhile in Europe in 1917 Gustov von Belo, a Pomeranian Army officer, experienced a profound and life-directing conversion as a result of an independent Bible study. He opened his home and began ministering. Soon the gifts of the Spirit, including tongues, appeared. Among these people, tongues were sung rather than spoken. People sang ''spiritual songs (Eph. 5:19) in languages unknown to the singers and recognized by the hearers.''

The Holiness Movement

The emergence of the ''holiness'' movement was an important part of the preparation of the development of the so-called Pentecostal movement of the twentieth century. Considerable concern for a deeper, higher or more intimate Christian life was the key to the teaching of such preachers and evangelists as John Wesley, A.B. Simpson, Dwight L. Moody, Reuben Torrey, Art Pierson, Hannah Whithall Smith, Frederick Brotherton Meyer and A.J. Gordon.

In 1896, revival came to North Carolina, Tennessee and Georgia. One group emerged to become the Church of God (Cleveland, Tennessee), the oldest Pentecostal denomination in America.

In 1880, reports of revival came from a Moravian mission outpost. Many were shaken and compelled to cry out for mercy as such gifts of the Holy Spirit as prophecy and tongues, together with visions and dreams, appeared among the wakened.

In Sweden in 1902 the late Lewi Pethrus, a young Baptist minister who had contact with the Salvation Army and Methodism, visited a group in Oslo who had experienced a healing ministry. Upon leaving them, Pethrus says, ''Tears streamed down my cheeks while I was overflowing with joy. A current of power and sweetness went through my entire being and I spoke strange words which surprised me a great deal.''

Pethrus left his Baptist pastorate to launch what became the largest church in Stockholm. This, in turn, spawned hundreds of other satellite congregations. It also founded a missionary society which today fields a thousand missionaries and has an extensive publication program.

Pentecostalism

Meanwhile, in 1900 a Methodist minister, Charles F. Parham, opened a Bible college in Topeka, Kansas, with forty students. These men and women, twelve of them ministers, had been asked to study informally the subject of baptism in the Holy Ghost while Parham was out of town preaching in December of that year. They did so, following his suggestion that they search the biblical passages for evidence of this baptism. On his return he was amazed to find that they had all reached the same conclusion: one evidence had come every time with the Holy Spirit in the Bible, and that was speaking in other tongues. The group began to wait expectantly, praying and meditating, and the Holy Spirit came upon them—first upon one and then upon several, and they spoke in tongues. This new phenomenon soon attracted attention, and newspapers in Kansas City and St. Louis reported what was happening.

The Parhams went on to Kansas City and to small towns in Kansas. In the spring of 1903, healings were first reported in his meetings. Then, two years later, the Parhams went to Texas. In Houston and a number of other cities the revival continued to grow. The experience of tongues was received by scores of people, and healings and other amazing experiences continued. In December, he established a Bible school in Houston, similar to the Topeka college. It was from here that Pentecostalism reached Los Angeles and began to mushroom.

DISCUSSION QUESTIONS

1. What do you think helped to change the minds and attitudes of men like Augustine and Martin Luther? What does this say to us about being willing to be open-minded in our

beliefs (Rom. 12:2-3)?

2. Consider Wesley's quote regarding "extraordinary circumstances." What types of things might prevent or hinder a person from being open to new evidences in the area of signs and wonders? How should we deal with an attitude of "closemindedness" (1 Thess. 5:12-23)?

3. Read Ephesians 4:2,3,30-32. What does this say to us, not only in reference to dealing with difficult brothers and sisters in Christ, but in our dealings with critical or hostile nonbelievers?

4. Historically, what were the results when gifts of the Spirit or some type of miracle took place (that is, 1896 in North Carolina, or what Lewi Pethrus did in Sweden)? Why do you think this was so?

APPLICATION

Read and discuss Acts 1:4-8 and Acts 2:1-21,41-47. What was the reason for this occurrence? What were the eventual results? How can this be applied to your ministry as a church and your lives as believers in Christ today?

This exclusive interview with a man who has become an evangelical legend in his time is a testimony to openness and honesty when faced with evidence which seems to contradict years of theological indoctrination.

7

Seeing Is Believing
by Donald A. McGavran

Donald A. McGavran is world famous as the father of the church growth movement. He has served as a missionary in India and has traveled mission fields of the world in his research on church growth. He was the founding dean of the School of World Mission, Fuller Theological Seminary. Before retiring from teaching at the age of 84, he regularly delivered a lecture on the subject of healing and church growth. This interview captures McGavran's thoughts on the subject.

Dr. McGavran, in a day when the evangelical community has largely ruled out signs and wonders, why is Fuller Seminary offering this course?

The entire church growth emphasis is concerned with obedience to the Great Commission. It is based on biblical convictions. Church growth is fundamentally a theological concept that those who are not believers, who do not believe in Jesus Christ, are lost. They are far from the heavenly Father's house. How do we appeal to them with the gospel of Jesus Christ?

I do not come from a church background that emphasizes healing. In fact, we have been a bit critical of it. Yet in my research I have discovered the winning of the lost has come in great numbers where men and women were healed in Christ's name. Amazing church growth has resulted.

Would you say that a ministry of healing in the name of Jesus Christ is the greatest cause of church growth?

There are many causes of church growth. In some cases there has been great church growth without any healing at all. But on the other hand, a great deal of church growth has taken place by virtue of healing campaigns of one sort or another. My first reaction to that discovery shocked me. The normal reaction of any ordinary American is, "Now wait a minute. If you're sick you go to a hospital."

The suggestion that you call somebody and have him or her anoint you with oil and pray over you often is regarded as a bit superstitious. Oh, we know it's in the Bible. And maybe in another dispensation, a long time ago, it worked. But not today. Now if you're sick you get a shot of penicillin. That's the typical reaction of the secular American; yes, of the secular American Christian. We're inclined to think that healing is charlatanism. It's a bit disreputable. It was from that point of view that I first had to face the issue.

How long ago was it that you first considered the possibility of healing as a means of church growth?

I've been thinking along these lines for maybe 10 or 15 years. But the evidence I uncovered in country after country—and in North America as well—simply wouldn't permit me to hold my former point of view. And I may say that as I meditated on it, my biblical conviction also wouldn't permit it. In other words, God is not helpless today. It is ridiculous to assume the only way He can heal is through injections or operations.

What was the reaction of your colleagues, Dr. McGavran, when you began to suggest that healing might be for today?

I don't know. But I would think my colleagues at first would have shared my revulsion at the idea. As they thought about it, however, I'm sure they would grant that the evidence for it is fairly strong. And the biblical principles which we profess here at Fuller certainly leave the door open. So these various things led me to the position that I now hold. That is, while God does cure through medical means, it also is true that God heals in answer to prayer. And if there is a psychosomatic process, and there is, then peoples' minds have a good deal to do with their healing. And if minds have a good deal to do with healing, then God, the Infinite Mind, has a good deal to do with healing.

So partly by a theological position and partly by the observation of evidence, I came to the conclusion that missionaries— as well as pastors and serious laymen and women—ought to regard healing much more openmindedly than they have. They must not narrowly shut themselves off in a corner and say, "That's not reputable," or "We would endanger our reputation."

That's a bit cowardly. We need to be braver than that. We need simply to face the fact that healing does occur, and that God uses healing to bring men and women to Christ.

What would you say about the other gifts of the Spirit enumerated in Corinthians and Romans?

I would say these are genuine gifts. God gives various gifts to pastors, evangelists, administrators. He gives some the gift of hospitality, some the gift of fluent speech and some the gift of administration. And He gives some the gift of healing.

Of the various aspects of church growth that you have explored, would you say that the manifestation of the Spirit of God in this way is responsible for 10 percent, 20 percent or more of conversions?

That depends on circumstances. In some places, it's responsible for 80 percent. Take, for example, in Brazil where the Assemblies of God have grown enormously to a community of approximately six million baptized believers. They count heavily on a ministry of healing. But other denominations have shared in the general responsiveness that has resulted from these healings. People pray for healings regularly. Not only do the pastors pray, but the laymen pray.

In Mexico City a short time ago, I was talking to a Swedish

missionary. I said to him, "Brother Anderson, I'm investigating why churches grow." One of the stories he told me was of his experience as a young missionary when he would go out on the streets and preach. One of his converts went along with him and would hand out tracts. Then his helper moved to another city.

Now when this layman got to the other city he said to himself, "What does a Christian do? Well, he goes out on the street and preaches." So he went out on the street and preached. But he wasn't a very good preacher and nobody listened to him.

So he asked himself, "Where do people go when they are sick?"

He answered, "They go to the drug store."

So he went to the drug store. And as people came out with a bottle of medicine in their hand, he would tap them on the shoulder and say, "Someone sick at your house?"

And they would say, "Yes."

"Would you like me to bring Someone who can heal them?"

And they would say, "Yes, of course."

So he would go and kneel down at the bedside and put his hand on the head of the person who was sick and pray in the name of Jesus for God to heal him. And God did. At the end of the first year he had a church of 26 believers.

Now that's a method of church growth I would never have thought about. And I expect that Anderson wouldn't have either. But that layman did. And God honored him.

So in Brazil, and in a good many other places in Latin America, the healing ministry has been an open door. And it has aided those denominations which do not believe in a healing ministry. It has made them more aware of and responsive to the power of God.

But you find other places where the healing ministry has not been used, yet where there is church growth. We must avoid thinking that the healing ministry is the only open door. It is not. God uses many methods. Our Lord used many methods. He healed, yes. But He also taught. So it is this total picture that we've got to see.

DISCUSSION QUESTIONS

1. What is the "Great Commission" McGavran speaks of? What can we do as individuals and as a group to fulfill this commission? How do signs and wonders come into play in this area? Identify the power promise in each of the following appearances of the Great Commission: Matt. 28:18-20; Mark 16:15-18; Luke 24:45-49; John 20:21-22; Acts 1:8.
2. Read the following scriptures: Matt. 9:1-8; John 2:23; Acts 5:12-16; Acts 10:36-42. What part did healing play in the growth of the churches and Christian believers?
3. Have you ever seen or experienced a healing? What were the circumstances?
4. If someone came to you, either in your group or to you alone, and asked for prayer for healing, what would you do? Would you know how to pray for them? Does your responsibility to that person end with the prayer or even with the healing?
5. Have you ever seen or experienced a manifestation of any of the spiritual gifts? How did you feel or react? Again, discuss what the purpose for these gifts is (1 Cor. 12:7; 1 Cor. 14:12; Eph. 4:11-12,13,16).

APPLICATION

1. Make a list of the gifts of the Spirit of which you are aware. Which of these gifts would be readily accepted in your church? Which would not be accepted at all? Why? What can you, as an individual believer and as a group, do to help in the acceptance of these gifts?
2. Discuss whether or not you believe it is important for the church to be open to these things. If the final decision is positive, then prayerfully consider what your responsibilities in this area are...and act on them.

Here, for the first time in print, is the lecture on healing that Donald McGavran presented to his Fuller Seminary students during the final few years of his teaching ministry.

8

Divine Healing and Church Growth

by Donald A. McGavran

The problem of church growth faces all of us. Many of us are working where we have had little. Where our churches are sealed off, ethnically, economically or educationally, the people from other classes of society do not ordinarily join us. For the last twenty-five years I have been studying church growth on the world scene. For twenty-five years before that I was studying it in the Indian context. So for about fifty years I have been considering the difficulty.

Evidence Is There

As I have been reviewing church growth around the world, I have seen that it frequently correlates with great healing campaigns. That is why I am addressing divine healing and church growth. Where the church is up against an insuperable barrier, there no matter what you do, how much you pray, how much you work, how much you organize, how much you administer for church growth, the church either does not grow, grows only a little, or grows from within, not from without. Under such circumstances, we need to lean heavily on that which is so wonderfully illustrated in the New Testament, namely the place of healing in church growth. I think of two villages of Lydda and Sharon where it is recorded in the book of Acts that all Lydda and Sharon turned to the Lord. Two whole villages in a day! When did it happen? When Aeneas was healed by Peter.

This great ingathering was preceded by a remarkable case of divine healing.

American missionaries, who have grown up in a highly secular society, usually take a dim view of divine healing, considering it mere charlatanism. After long years of sharing that common opinion, I now hold that among vast populations, divine healing is one of the ways in which God brings men and women to believe in the Savior. Missiologists ought to have a considered opinion on the matter. They should not brush it off cheaply and easily. Administering for church growth in part means arranging the stage so that divine healing can take place. Look at the evidence of divine healing. Withhold judgment until the evidence has been reviewed. There is much more evidence than I am able to present in one short chapter.

My considered recommendation is that missionaries and Christians in most populations ought to be following the biblical injunction to pray for the sick (James 5:14-15). When notable healings have taken place, great efforts should be made to multiply churches. When healings have taken place in your denomination, when some Pentecostals mount a great healing campaign, then say to yourself, "This is the time to strike, while the iron is hot."

Presbyterians in India

I now want to examine a few cases of divine healing that have come to my attention from various sources. The first is a case of healing carried out by American Presbyterian missionaries. I quote a report from India about the operation of these ministers, visiting India for a brief period:

Everyday there was preaching in the evening and teaching in the morning. They lived with us as brothers. They visited and preached in 24 of the 278 churches we have. The work of the Holy Spirit was experienced throughout the preaching ministry. Dick Little was blessed with the gift of healing power. All those who came to the gospel meetings with a real longing for healing were wonderfully healed. Every night Little had to minister for more than four hours. People who were healed came forward and witnessed about their healing. Hundreds of people were healed. Thousands were able to accept Jesus Christ as their Lord. People were made whole physically, mentally and spiritually. Some of our pastors were healed from serious illnesses. Those who were suffering from chronic diseases were healed. A woman who was suffering from asthma for twenty-one years was healed. A man who was deaf for more than forty years was healed. So many blind people were able to see. Lame people were healed. People who were suffering from bleeding were healed. Wilson shared how more than two weeks after Little had departed, he would visit a church and find people still praising God for the healing they had received. He discovered that there were a number of Hindus who had received Jesus Christ as their Lord and Savior among the thousands who experienced salvation. It was customary for Dick Little to ask the people to renounce their gods before repenting and accepting the Lord Jesus into their lives. Apparently a number received their healing as Christ Jesus came into their hearts.

Anglicans in Tanzania

The second comes from the CMS newsletter. This is written by the general secretary of the famed Church Missionary Society whose headquarters are just across the Thames from the Parliament Building in London. Here is what was published:

Perhaps there is no more impressive example in recent years of healing than Edmond John, younger brother of the archbishop of Tanzania, with his great healing missions over a three-year period of ministry from 1972 to 1975. Not only were vast numbers of people healed, exorcised, moved to open repentance, led to or brought back to Christ in great gatherings, but also in quiet, ordered proceedings. All that happened was related to the central apprehension that Jesus is Lord; an amazing response for the lax Christians and the newly drawn Muslims alike. John's death at the end of the astonishing blaze of ministry to his people left behind in many places a church spiritually and numerically strengthened.

Methodists in Bolivia

The third is from Bolivia, from a United Methodist. This man studied at our School of World Mission and went back to Bolivia a convinced church growth man. His letter is addressed to me personally. In it he says:

It is most striking that the district of our church which has really broken new ground in growth is our very own Lake District where we have worked for sixteen years. This is the rural Aymara Indian district. This growth really began to gather momentum during our absence and has been strongest during the last year. So new is this that we do not yet have proper statistics on what has taken place. The mother church of the district in Ancoraimes, our mission station, has increased its Sunday morning attendance six fold. They hold weekly meetings that have usually averaged 250 and this year have averaged over 600. For the first time in the history of our work, a majority approaching consensus has turned to Christ in a single community; practically the whole village became Christian. This was shown dramatically on May 31, 1973, the traditional fiesta date, when the community celebrated their first community Christian Fiesta. Of the 170 families, 160 have turned to Christ, five out of six zones of the community, which is called Turini. The lay pastor of the Ancoraimes church, Juan Cordero, was the key man in this movement. Now mum's the word, please do not say anything about this, Dr. McGavran; mum's the word on the following factor: preaching has been accompanied by healing! Over and over this has been the case. The lay pastor has been practically mobbed on occasion, but he has stood his ground and has virtually obliged interested persons to hear him out on the gospel before he will pray for healings.

India and Ethiopia

The fourth case of healing followed by growth is one in which the gift of healing was exercised by a layperson, a recent convert, not by the minister or missionary. In Tamilnadu, India, the Evangelical Church of India, planted by OMS of Greenwood, Indiana, has grown from a few hundred in 1966 to more than 15,000 in 1982. During 1983 this church expects to plant fifty more churches—one a week.

After 1970 growth was accompanied by healings and

exorcisms. What convinced multitudes to follow Christ was that with their own eyes they saw men and women healed by Christ's mighty power. Evil spirits were driven out in His name. The Holy Spirit was at work.

The fifth is from the Mekane Yesus Lutheran denomination in Ethiopia. "Eighty-three percent of our congregation give healing from illness and exorcism as reasons for their growth."

In summary, it is clear from these five cases and much more evidence that the growth of the church has often—not always, but often—been sparked by healing campaigns.

The Missionary Doctor

During the last 100 years, Western Christians have been heavily secularized and saturated with scientific thinking. They believe diseases are caused, not by God's will, but by germs. And these diseases are cured by drugs; malaria by quinine, colds by Contac, atherosclerosis by open heart surgery. As Christianity has spread throughout the world, missionary physicians have proved enormously more effective than the mumbo jumbo of witch doctors, herbalists, faith healers of the animist world. The missionary doctor gave the patients penicillin and offered prayer to God for their cure. They were cured.

The Christian doctor would say it was not by unaided prayer but by using the medicine that God has given to mankind. This Christian interpretation of the healing process and the part played by unaided prayer and faith differs from the rationalist's view, and yet it holds that, as a matter of fact, God does not act independently of physical means. That, my friends, is the atmosphere in which we all live. Secularists believe that there is no god; the causes of illness which can be measured and manipulated by humans are the only reality. These causes can be physical, chemical or psychological.

To such twentieth-century thinking, faith healing is at best mistaken and at worst charlatanry. The faith healer is either a self-deluded enthusiast or a clever manipulator. If people claim to be cured, maybe they were not really sick in the first place, or have temporary feelings of well-being induced by the excitement of the moment due to crowd psychology. The "healed" may even be planted by the faith healer to build up his or her reputation. The power of hundreds of thousands who believe alike and express their belief vividly is a real factor in human affairs and has been used by politicians, merchants, priests and magicians from time immemorial. Westerners and Eastern secularists alike are highly skeptical about any power available other than what human beings themselves generate by one means or another. Faith healing causes lifted eyebrows and superior smiles.

Can Spirits Cause Disease?

To most people in Asia, Africa and Latin America, however, disease is inflicted by spirits. It is cured by super-human power, regardless of what people in America think.

People in the Third World are convinced that witches eat up the life force of other people. An angry neighbor casts an "evil eye" on a woman and she grows weaker day by day. A wandering evil spirit devours a baby and the baby dies. A demon causes an illness which no medicine can cure. Western medicine may help some people, but Africa is full of mysterious powers which the white man does not know, and only those who know the secret source of black power can heal African affliction. These evil powers must be overcome by superior powers.

In Spanish America the curandero has great power. His incantations, potion, sacrifices and medicines marvelously heal the sick. In Asia, Africa and Latin America, perhaps ninety-eight out of every 100 persons believe that superior power drives out inferior power. Even in Europe and North America the impersonal, mechanistic system of scientism fails to satisfy millions. Therefore, they, too, eagerly believe in the occult, extra-human powers. Satan-worship flourishes. The mysterious influence of magic words, rites, robes, stars, yoga and gurus fascinates many people in Europe and North America. But Christians in North America and Europe have a special problem with faith healing. Why? Because their religion wars with their science.

Healing in the New Testament

Faith healing unquestionably occurred in biblical times. The

New Testament church rode the crest of a tremendous, continuous manifestation of faith healing. One of the many passages reads as follows:

Now many signs and wonders were done among the common people and by the hands of the apostles, more than ever, believers were added to the Lord. Multitudes, both men and women, so that they even carried out the sick into the streets and laid them on beds and pallets, that, as Peter came by, at least his shadow might fall on some of them. The people also gathered from the towns around Jerusalem, bringing the sick and those afflicted with evil spirits and they all were healed (Acts 8:12-16).

Divine healing was an essential part of the evangelization as churches multiplied across Palestine and the Mediterranean world. What are we Christians to make of all this? Is there something here that we can use?

Many educated Christians have been more secularized than they realize and are antagonistic to divine healing. They write it off, superstition and fraud; it leads people away from sound medicine and counts many as healed who are still sick. They say divine healing is a massive deception. They think that divine healing is using God for our own ends.

Some educated Christians say that in addition to the human mechanism and material means which God uses, He sometimes acts with sovereign power. He retains the right to act outside His laws which we know in order to use higher laws which we do not know. He ordinarily operates through His laws, but He is not bound by them. When it pleases Him, He intervenes. Such Christians hold that the best possible world is one in which most of the time a just and loving God rules through laws. But occasionally, when He sees fit, He uses the higher law. Such Christians view healings in the name of Christ as demonstrations of the power of God.

Some would add that the healings are a mixture of God's acts and human acts, thus we see many incomplete healings, and failures of healings, due to the lack of faith or sincerity.

Seeing Is Believing

Some hard-headed Christians, who would normally be highly skeptical about divine healing, have gradually come to accept healing campaigns upon seeing the great numbers who throw away crutches, plus those healed of deafness and blindness and cured of heart disease. They have seen large numbers of recent nonbelievers rejoicing at Christ's power, singing His praises, hearing His word and praying to Him. The *facts* overwhelm the hard-headed.

Finally, some Christians believe that God has called them to engage actively in healing the sick, exorcising evil spirits and multiplying churches. They deliberately use the vigorous expressed faith in Christ which abounds in a healing campaign to multiply sound churches of responsible Christians.

All Christians ought to think their way through this matter and realize that here is a power which a great many of us have not sufficiently used.

Christian leaders from England, China, Indonesia, Kenya, Nigeria, Guatemala, Ivory Coast and South Africa, all from the Fuller School of World Mission, share exciting experiences from their personal ministries.

9

Around the World

Some years ago Loren Cunningham, head of the missionary organization Youth With a Mission, was asked to speak in a Seoul, Korea, church. He was surprised to be greeted by a congregation of 6,000.

At last count, Paul Yonggi Cho's Yoido Full Gospel Church had upwards of 500,000 members. Growth rate is approximately one new baptized member every seven minutes.

That church, along with another in the same city with a membership of 80,000, presents Jesus Christ as provider for all the needs of man—material and spiritual—including physical healing.

Meanwhile, in nations around the world, similar evidence of the power of God in signs and wonders is being demonstrated. In Latin America, the spiritual renewal began in the 1950s with the astonishing proliferation of the Pentecostal movement— particularly in Chile, Brazil and Colombia, but also in other countries.

In Africa, stemming from the faithful witness of early denominational missions and missionaries, a charismatic-style revival emerged through national churches and denominations. Latest figures put the number of independent denominations at roughly 8,000.

A similar explosion in church growth is taking place in Asia today as a result of demonstrations of the revival and healing power of God.

The reports which follow are not presented as in-depth studies of any given area. Instead, they are testimonies of students at Fuller Theological Seminary, most of them nationals of Third World countries. They serve as eyewitness observers of the emergence of signs and wonders as a viable tool of the Holy Spirit in bringing men and women to faith in Jesus Christ today.

England

"You don't need to hold my arm any more. I can see where I am going," an old lady kneeling at the communion rail protested to the dumbfounded members of her family.

Now a year later the same woman, once blinded by a detached retina in one eye and a cataract in the other, continues to express her gratitude to God for her restored sight and His presence in her life.

The church which witnessed this work of God was St. Andrew's Church, Chorleywood—an upper-middle-class parish twenty-eight miles north of London. The occasion was the visit of John Wimber from Vineyard Christian Fellowship, Anaheim, California, during Pentecost weekend 1981.

It was but one of a string of equally remarkable happenings, including a medical doctor healed of a bowel and liver infection and a multiple sclerosis sufferer who, for the first time in four years, rose from her wheelchair and exchanged places with her husband, pushing him around the church in her chair. As the people packing the church became aware of what was happening, they forgot their English reserve, jumped to their feet (with some even standing on the pews to get a better view) and applauded her progress along the church aisles.

At St. Michael-le-Belfrey in York, the Lord also manifested His presence in powerful ways. John Wimber had been invited by David Watson for a special time of ministry. The church magazine reported, "It seems that almost everyone met with God during that memorable week." But, of course, such unscheduled events have caused alarm as well as rejoicing.

England, in common with the rest of Western Europe, has seen the church decline alarmingly in attendance throughout the past seventy years. But the church scene today is not one of gloom and despondency. Far from it. The Holy Spirit is moving through the churches enlivening worship and spilling across denominational boundaries. As a result, a turn in the tide of church attendance has spawned a number of house church groupings.

There now is a deepening recognition that the Spirit's work is not only to help us cope with the spontaneous but also with the supernatural. His working in power is not confined to delighting the saints but to empowering them for effective witness in the world. Many who have become consumers and connoisseurs of "charismatic" ministry are being challenged themselves to minister to others in the Spirit's power.

Malcolm Widdecombe of the Anglican church of St. Philip and Jacob, Bristol, tells of the Spirit bringing blessing as the church learned to seek first the kingdom of God. In 1963 the church, which had dwindled to an evening attendance of 35, was threatened with closure by the bishop. Today it has an average evening attendance of 250. Members give sacrificially, and the church itself demonstrates its dependence on God to meet material needs by giving away to missions two thirds of its total income!

Gerald Coates, leader of the 400-strong Cobham Christian Fellowship, reports that 500 people (a conservative estimate) either came to Christ for the first time or were filled with the Spirit on a recent Sunday night in Edinburgh. The fellowship links together a number of house groups in Cobham, Surrey, which is part of commuter-land for London.

Nigel Wright, a Baptist minister in Lytham St. Annes near Blackpool, reports that over half his congregation of 250 has been filled with the Spirit and many healed.

In Peterborough, Roy Pointer, the Bible Society's church growth consultant, tells of the deaf hearing and the partially paralyzed finding a new mobility. He writes, "Many of the experiences recorded in the New Testament were found in

Peterborough that night.''

EDDIE GIBBS, *an ordained Anglican minister and former missionary to Chile, is now assistant professor of church growth at Fuller Theological Seminary.*

China

According to Donald G. Barnhouse, in his 1950 *China Report*: "If you want to see the power of God, the atmosphere must be one of great difficulty. If you want to see the miracle power of God, it must be one of impossibility. Difficulty has been changed to impossibility in China...and it would seem that our Lord loves to work under such circumstances; and there is every evidence that He is doing so." In the following interview with David Wang, these evidences are shown to be as real today as they were when Barnhouse wrote his report. Wang, a graduate of the Fuller School of World Mission, is a native of Shanghai and general director of Asian Outreach.

David, would you tell us some of the incidents which you think validate the fact that God is working today in China?

Let me just share with you one of my latest visits to China, in September 1981. I was able to visit the province of Inner Mongolia, which has been closed to visitors for a long time.

I stayed with a woman minister there. She was a graduate of a Bible school in China, and was, in fact, deported to Inner Mongolia because she refused to deny her Christian faith.

When she first came to Mongolia, she met a party secretary. He was the local "king" there, assigned from Peking. His wife was ill. He went to this woman and asked her to take care of his wife, to try to heal her. The woman doctor tried, but found that the secretary's wife wasn't responding well to medication. Finally, one day, she asked the wife if she would mind if she prayed for her. She said, "No, I will try anything to get well." So the doctor gathered together a number of Christians and they prayed for her. And God healed her.

That woman became a secret follower of Christ. Since then,

rather than putting pressure on the Christians or trying to stop their expansion, the secretary has just closed his eyes to their activities.

So this woman started a church along with her medical practice?

That's right. And because of that particular healing, the doctor was given the special privilege of traveling to various towns and villages in Inner Mongolia. Now she has a congregation of 1,200 people. I stayed with her for about three nights and four days. Almost every night she would have people coming into her home, from all over Mongolia. Some people rode bicycles for days just to see what was happening. Again and again she would lead them in a prayer of repentance. She would teach them the way of salvation.

So signs and wonders are not uncommon in Inner Mongolia. Particularly power encounters. I recall a situation that involved a group of Christians. There were around forty of us at a house meeting. A woman told us how she and her son were deserted by her husband. They had to move because they couldn't survive in their native village anymore. When they arrived here they couldn't find any place to stay. The local president finally took them to a deserted house and let them stay there.

After about a week, the president asked them if everything was OK.

"Yes," the lady told him, "we are very grateful for this place to stay."

"Nothing bothering you?"

"No, nothing at all," she said. The president then told her that the house had been haunted for generations. It was a famous "ghost place," and no one even dared to walk by it at night.

Then the president asked the woman and her son, since their God was so good, if they would come and pray for a woman who had been demon-possessed for years. She was so violent that she was kept chained up in a small room.

The woman agreed to pray for her but asked for some time to prepare. She went back to her native village, gathered a number of Christians together, then came back and told the president that they were ready to pray for the demon-possessed woman. They were taken to her hut. Crowds gathered around to watch. About a half hour later, the Christians came out and asked for some water for washing and some clothes. An hour or so after that, they came out again, this time with the woman completely cured, totally healed. That brought about a phenomenal number of conversions in that village.

How long is it since the gospel has been preached in China?

In 1949, Chairman Mao Tse-tung expelled almost all missionaries from China. Chinese pastors were "liquidated" or sent to labor camps. Church buildings and Christian institutes were converted into warehouses, schools and factories. Some were simply closed off and left to decay. By 1959, over eighty percent of the churches in China were closed. And in a 1970 report, it was noted that some twenty percent of the thirty-five to sixty-five million deaths caused by the Communist regime were directly related to religious faith. When the missionaries were expelled from China, there were an estimated four million believers in China. Today there is sufficient evidence to show that there could be as many as twenty-five to fifty million Christian believers there.

Signs and wonders not only are bringing Christians into the kingdom, but they probably are the determining factor in helping Chinese Christians preserve their faith. With no Bibles, missionaries, pastors or churches, and little fellowship since they were still in a repressive cultural revolution, we wondered what sustained them. Probably it has been signs and wonders.

I learned of one woman whose daughter had worked in a quarry. She was in charge of the work shifts. When she blew a whistle, the workers would come up out of the mines. One day she was working in her office and she heard a voice calling her by name, telling her that she should blow the whistle to let the workers come out of the mines. There was still another hour before she was supposed to do this, but she repeatedly heard this voice, telling her to blow the whistle now. Finally, without checking with the other members of the office because she feared they would stop her, she blew the whistle. The miners started coming out. No sooner had the last one left the mines than an earthquake caved in several of the mines. If the workers had still been in the mines, the death toll would have been staggering.

The miners gathered around this girl and asked why she had blown the whistle early. She had to admit that she was a Christian and that she had just obeyed the voice of God. Hundreds accepted the Lord that day. Then, at an official inquiry, she gave a powerful testimony and many more families accepted Christ.

One Christian leader inside China told us that, because they were not able to read the Bible or hear messages preached from the pulpit, the Lord seemed to be comforting them and directing them very often, through dreams and visions.

Then there are recorded testimonies of angels guarding house churches while their persecutors came to arrest them. Upon seeing what they described as "soldiers dressed in white" surrounding these churches, the persecutors fled. Some even turned to Christ.

So, David, you are saying that of all the means available for church growth in China today, that you believe the demonstration of the gifts of the Spirit is the most significant and effective factor?

Yes.

How are you going to get around the belief that those gifts aren't available for today?

When you are driven into a corner where you have no theology to turn to, when you have no denomination to go to, and there are no other straws to hang on to, you have to go back to the basic foundation. And that is the power of God.

What we are seeing today inside China is a people movement. Very often a whole village comes to Christ. Stanley Mooneyham, author and mission leader, recorded an interview with a young girl who told him that of the 100 families in her village, eighty were believers in Christ. This was due to one particular healing miracle.

Then there is the Jesus Mountain, located in the Southern province near Canton. The majority of the commune members who live there are Christians. They are firm believers in Christ, and they call themselves the Jesus Brigades. They work alongside the other brigades, Communists, and outperform everybody. They also have the highest moral and ethical standards. Even the Communist party members hold them up as an example to other workers. These believers came into being because of the healings and exorcisms that they experienced.

I think China can be reached for God only through God's power. If the Lord allows us to go back to China, we must be a partner in the work of the Holy Spirit. We must not say that these things don't happen anymore. That is what some Three-Self church leaders inside China are saying. That is what they are publishing and printing in the magazines of the official church...that signs and wonders ceased with the apostles, that they are not for today. This has been creating confusion and division among the believers in China.

This is an area we really need to pray about.

Do you believe that the principles you use in China are applicable in the other countries in which you work?

I don't know if this is accurate, but I believe that the Asian church is much more open to the work of the Holy Spirit. There are churches like Paul Yonggi Cho's church in Korea which has a membership of more than a half million. In this church signs, wonders and healings happen regularly. And the church is growing rapidly.

Those of us who have been exposed to Western scientific theology or to a Western worldview find it difficult to believe in signs, wonders and miracles. In fact, some of the Asian and Chinese students at Fuller have said, "We've never seen it in our lives. Our church never talks about the gifts of the Spirit. We've never heard a sermon on this line, or seen anything like that.'' So I pray that more and more of the Third World people can develop an indigenous theology along the line of signs, wonders and the power of God.

And when we, as missionaries, confront this kind of culture, it will be absolutely essential for us to demonstrate the power of our God. We should be in tune to what these people with this kind of background—people from Asia, Africa, Korea, Indonesia—have to offer us.

Indonesia

David and Eva Brougham have been missionaries in Southeast Asia, working through the Indonesian Missionary Fellowship. He is an evangelist, she a physician. Both are Bible teachers and graduates of the Fuller School of World Mission. They are Presbyterian, and their theological training is strongly grounded in conservative, dispensational evangelicalism. They did not believe that miracles could occur today. They did not believe that healing and deliverance were meant for the present. To them, these things happened in Jesus' lifetime, but not now.

Yet their experiences on the mission field contradicted the theory they had learned in the seminary classrooms.

They saw people healed. They saw people delivered from demon oppression. They saw people experience a special, second blessing from the Holy Spirit. The Broughams witnessed God working in the world today.

David and Eva decided they needed to re-learn their theology, to correlate their theology with their experiences. They heard about Fuller's course on signs, wonders and church growth, and decided to become involved.

In the following interview, the Broughams relate their experiences in the course and from the mission field.

What is your evaluation of this course, MC510?

David: We've taken over a hundred credit units at Fuller Seminary in various kinds of church growth and theological courses since 1968. But this course distinguished itself from other church growth courses. Instead of concentrating on theory, we put the classroom theory to practical demonstration by participating in the healing ministry of churches.

Didn't you also participate in this kind of ministry on the mission field?

David: Yes, we did.

So you look at the gospel as a wholistic gospel of spiritual salvation and physical deliverance?

Eva: Exactly. I came into mission work when I started to study medicine with the purpose of serving the Lord. So there is no problem in my mind that the Lord deals with the whole person, physically and spiritually. I couldn't be a physician without praying for sick people. The medical help is definitely secondary and often depends on the circumstances. If I have good medicine and good equipment I can do only what I have learned in the hospital. But if I don't have these things what can I do except call upon the name of the Lord?

But haven't you been working with institutions that not only would not be interested in this approach, but might even assert that it is not a part of the gospel?

David: Yes, we have worked in conservative evangelical institutions in Singapore and in the Philippines. Because of their worldview and their understanding of the gospel, they have emphasized two very good things brought out in Matthew 9:35. That is, that Jesus went about all the cities and villages teaching in their synagogues and preaching and proclaiming the good news of the kingdom.

But the third aspect of Jesus' ministry is in Matthew 9:35 also, "curing all kinds of disease and every weakness and infirmity." This is from the Amplified version. This has been put in the corner. It's something that may happen, but nobody talks about it. You have to talk out in the backyard if you want to talk about how demons have been cast out.

We trust now with the new attitude coming into evangelical circles, starting here at Fuller, that there will be a new openness toward the healing ministry of Jesus.

Why do you think there has been this reluctance on the part of so many?

David: It's because we have been brought up with the idea that everything is done by a naturalistic order. In other words, we don't really understand the realm of the spirit. Anything we can't perceive with our senses, anything that is not according to the scientific method, we cannot accept as reality.

Most of our Asian theologians have been trained by Western theologians. So they do not reflect an Asian worldview which is more open to the mystical spirit world. They somehow haven't found the counterpart in the Christian faith.

So I think it is because of that kind of emphasis in our Western seminaries. It's our over-reliance on natural order instead of a supernatural worldview that says God is here today and He can break through time and space when He wants to touch someone. This is part of my explanation.

Eva: Another reason is that evangelicals are very cautious about the Pentecostal churches and the charismatic movement. Cautious is a moderate word. Sometimes evangelicals are very negative. They are afraid something might not be right according to the Scriptures.

And there is still a strong dispensational view that eliminates the possibility that God can do something supernatural today.

You mentioned that you would like to introduce such a course in your school. What school is that?

David: We have been assigned to the Indonesian Missionary Fellowship graduate school in East Java, Indonesia. They are hoping to establish a school next year for theology and mission. Their leader is Petros Octavianus, of the Indonesian Missionary Fellowship. He has participated in seeing people healed and in planting churches in Sumatra. He is considered by some the Billy Graham of Indonesia.

Has it been necessary for you to unlearn any prejudices or presuppositions that you held? Or to change your thinking in any way?

David: What I did not learn until I got into hard difficult situations on the field was that God is alive and working today. So my dispensational views had to undergo some changes. I saw things that happened in the Bible happening today. I had to go back and rethink my theology, especially concerning the person and work of the Holy Spirit.

I've come to realize that Jesus' works and words are still applicable today as they were yesterday.

Theologically, do you have any problem with the frequent mention of the baptism of the Holy Spirit?

Eva: No, we have reconciled this concept with the evangelical background that we are baptized in the Spirit when we are converted. But there is a constant need of a new filling. The Lord emphasized to us the need of enduement with power for service as it says in Acts 1:8, "Ye shall receive power after that the Holy Spirit is come upon you and you shall be witnesses unto me in Jerusalem, in Judea and unto the uttermost part of the earth."

We always tell our students, who are usually in an evangelical framework, "Yes, you are born again by the Holy Spirit, but you need a constant enduement with power."

David: I think if we look below the surface of historical evangelical theology, we will find that some of our spiritual heroes like Finney, Moody and Torrey had a second encounter with the Holy Spirit. Regardless of the terminology, which is useless to quibble over, they had another kind of enduement of the Spirit for their ministry.

Now there may be different manifestations, and we don't agree with all the brethren on what these are, but there will be some manifestations of the person of Jesus and spiritual gifts.

I know it is controversial. We've listened to various viewpoints, and it is a hang-up for some. But we believe we can give clear enough teaching from the Scriptures that people will realize being born again is not sufficient to go out and encounter the enemy in power.

Eva: We have some very fine friends in Asia, young people, who have gone through the Bible college where we taught. Outside the college they came into another experience with the Lord, and He is using them mightily. They are planting more churches than we could ever plant. They are bringing many people to Christ, praying for the sick and casting out demons. So I think the Lord has proven to us that it works.

Kenya

When is the last time you consulted a witch doctor for an illness or sacrificed an animal in gratitude to a god for a prayer request? Such actions may seem ludicrous to us with our modern-day mind-set. But to the people of Africa, the power of demons and witch doctors is evident and acknowledged widely. Jackson Mutie Munyao, a pastor of an Africa Inland Church in Kenya and a graduate of the Fuller School of World Mission, here emphasizes the importance of not only recognizing the powers of demons, but of resisting them through the power of the living God—even today.

For Africans, belief in Christ is not hard. They are used to responding on a supernatural level. But they are confused when white men, whom they feel are very knowledgeable, preach the gospel yet are unable to answer simple questions relating to the power encounters and spiritual struggles common to Africa.

Such a lack of knowledge and understanding on the part of Westerners has led many Christians in Africa to backslide. They could not understand how something extremely easy for the witch doctor—such as casting out demons—was virtually impossible for the learned missionary. When the missionaries could not help them in these issues, the people went back to the witch doctors in secret. After they had received healing from these witch doctors, they would offer a sacrifice to the pagan gods, then attend church the next day.

This problem arose because the work of the Holy Spirit in the area of healing and wonders too often has been overlooked. To Africans, the physical body means a lot. They will pay anything to receive healing, even if it means abandoning their Christianity. Because of this, the church is considered by many to be a place for resting or talking to one's neighbors. The God of the Christians, they reason, lives so far away He cannot understand what is happening in their lives.

How I Changed

Yet, more and more, the presence of the Holy Spirit is being seen in our churches. I come from the Africa Inland Church of Kenya, where we have been taught that signs and wonders do not happen today. And this is what I believed, until a member of our church became sick in 1963.

This man, Mutemi Mwinzi, was stricken by a strange illness which none of the doctors seemed able to treat or relieve. Soon, in spite of prayer and medication, and in spite of his consulting a witch doctor, it was decided that he probably would die soon. From that moment, he was left on his own. His family and friends would not care for him and came by each day only to see if he had died.

Mutemi, who knew a few verses in the Bible, remembered Psalm 27:10 which said, "My father and mother have abandoned me, but the Lord will take care of me." He spent a lot of time quoting that verse and talking to God, asking for help. Finally, one day he decided to drag himself outside to die. When he was about ten yards from his hut, he asked God either to heal him or let him die. And he promised God that, if he were healed, he would spend the rest of his life serving Him and would give all that he had to the church.

Suddenly Mutemi's body began to shiver. He fainted. When he woke up, his sickness was gone. He felt hungry and was able to walk back into his house to find some food. When his family and friends found him sitting and eating, he told them what had happened.

The following Sunday, Mutemi told his story to a church full of people. Many went forward to receive Christ, and the whole church experienced a revival. Mutemi, who was very rich by village standards, then promised to be responsible for the pastor's salary, and to build a new church. Men and women came from far and wide to hear the story. Within a year, the membership of this church grew from fifty to 300. Today, it still is growing. This was the first Africa Inland Church to start practicing healing for the sick, and God has blessed them.

Politics and the Holy Spirit

Some government and political people also experienced the power of God. One man, a politician from Rwanda, had been elected president of his party. This was to be his fourth term. Shortly before the elections, however, he had become a Christian, and God had told him that he was to leave politics. When he told the other members of the party this, they became upset and finally informed him that if he didn't accept the position that he, with all his family, animals and possessions would be burned. He had ten days to consider the situation.

When the ten days were up, the politician stood firm on his decision to follow God and leave politics. The whole council of elders gathered together and sent for the man. They read the charges against him and gave him one final chance to accept office. Again he refused. They all rushed at him and took him back to his home. He and his family were put inside the house. A crowd had gathered to watch, and they began preparing the fire to throw at his house. Suddenly, a great thunder and lightning storm struck down the crowd. Many men and women died on the spot. The parliament building was demolished. When the man looked out to see what was happening, he saw countless men and women lying around his compound, dead. The survivors were running away.

The man left politics with no further problems and went to work for the Lord, going from place to place preaching the gospel. Many people came to the Lord through his preaching, and a great revival was experienced.

All of these things have shown us very clearly that the power of the Holy Spirit is working in our land today.

Those of us who have experienced God's power need to speak up about what we have seen the Lord do and what we have heard of His doing for others. We must allow the Spirit of God to do His work. Then we shall rejoice, as the apostles did, having their same boldness in proclaiming the living gospel of Christ.

Nigeria

I was brought up in a denomination that does not want to hear anybody claiming that he or she can exercise the gift of healing today. Many of us grew up with that concept. We forget that God promised us that if we have faith as small as a ''mustard seed'' we will be able to do many wonderful things, which I believe include healing.

For the past five years, I suffered from backaches and had pain in my chest for three years. But one Monday evening in February this year, after having sat through my philosophical theology class for two hours, I said to myself, ''Why can't I go to this class on signs and wonders and test the professor? If it is true that God heals, as I was told, I shall see it.''

So I asked God to help me and give me the courage to be able to stand up before the class and tell them that I needed healing.

To my surprise, when the invitation to receive healing was given, I saw one of the professors, Peter Wagner, whom I respect very much, stand up.

I said to myself, ''Look at him asking for healing. Why do I have to waste my time saying that I am an evangelical believer and do not trust that God can use anybody today in a healing ministry?''

When I went to the front of the classroom, professor John Wimber immediately started praying. He asked God to give me faith to believe that I was going to be healed. I really felt something within me. I went home but not completely healed. After a few days, however, the pain left me completely.

Not only was my backache cured, but my chest was as well. The following day I went to have an X-ray of my chest. After the doctor examined the pictures, he told me he did not see anything wrong. I knew the Person who removed the trouble from me. It was the Lord Jesus who did it.

Why do we have to doubt what the Holy Spirit can do through people today? We are Christians. This means ''Christlike.'' If we are like Christ, why then can't we have faith in Christ— believing that He will use us through that ministry? Why do we not have faith that the person prayed for will be healed?

My only word of caution to those who have the gift of healing is to copy the example of Peter (and the rest who had that gift as recorded in the Scriptures) to always give glory to God. The only fault in a person God uses for healing is pride and claiming the glory for himself or herself.

My church seems not to understand the gifts of the Holy Spirit. I was brought up in an environment that claimed the gifts of the Holy Spirit, especially healing and speaking in tongues, probably don't apply to our own age today.

When somebody is sick in my church we say, "Let's pray for him." But our problem is this. We can only say, "Let's pray for the person." But we don't have enough faith to claim that God is going to heal the person.

I'm going back to Nigeria with a different concept as far as that is concerned. There is no need for the church to doubt that God can still use people today in healing. So that is one of the things I will go back to Nigeria with. Let the people understand that God is still alive. God healed people while He was here in the person of Jesus Christ. Even before Christ came, the prophets were doing wonderful things, even raising people from the dead. Today we must have that faith to claim His power in our lives.

DAWUDA MAIGARI *is principal of the Evangelical Church of West Africa Bible College, Kagoro, Nigeria.*

Guatemala

In 1965, in the city of Santa Rosa, Guatemala, there was a great drought. Cows were dying. Dogs were dying. People were leaving. Businesses went bankrupt. Crops were perishing. The government and civilian organizations tried to bring water in, but it was scarce in other places as well.

Religious leaders, of course, did their best. One particular group held Mass. They cried, did penance and everything else they could—but water would not come down. Evangelicals also were concerned. They prayed, "Oh, God, let the rain come.

We're perishing.''

Then it happened. In a small Pentecostal meeting, where some believers from the Principe de Paz churches had assembled for the regular worship service, the Spirit of the Lord moved in a mighty way. From one section of the church, a message in tongues came forth; a few moments later, the interpretation of those tongues: "Dig a well in the pastor's backyard. There you'll find water.''

There was much opposition from other churches as the deacons, elders and pastor began to dig. They thought these people were fanatics and/or were hallucinating—especially when they saw that the pastor's backyard was on a hill. A well is never dug on a hill because water runs low. But the pastor, deacons and elders continued to dig. Soon one of the deacons became quite upset.

"Why is it in the pastor's backyard? Why couldn't it be in my backyard?" asked one.

Another elder also thought that maybe the prophecy was biased.

One deacon left. One elder left. But there still remained a group obsessed with the idea that "just maybe" God would work it out for them.

Because of the drought, the land was hard, so the digging progressed slowly. On the fourth day they encountered a big boulder. It was so large they thought they had hit solid rock. The disappointments and frustrations were evident, as another elder left the shoveling team.

But they kept digging around the boulder until finally, after two days, they were able to remove it. As they did so, a gush of water came forth. It was so rich and plenteous, so sweet that they began to drink and drink.

The deacons and elders who had left came back to the church repenting with tears, thanking God for His promise and apologizing to those whom they had thought were "in the flesh." And the whole town came to the well. Since the pastor's backyard was the only place they could find water, it became one of the greatest places to lead people to Christ. A deacon and an elder were always right next to the well, helping the people with the water. And they would always say, "He who drinks of this water shall thirst again, but he who drinks of the water that Christ gives shall never thirst again."

What the miracle of the well did to the growth of this church carries on to this day. The number of conversions to Christ was staggering; the entire town was revolutionized. Membership grew from a few dozen to over 900 within that same year. And if you were to go to Santa Rosa, you also could drink of this water!

ENRIQUE ZONE *is president of the Facultad de Teologia of Montebello, California. Zone holds the M.A. in missiology from the Fuller School of World Mission.*

Ivory Coast

In a coastal village of the Ivory Coast, villagers gathered to listen to a man dressed in a white robe. He wore a white turban on his head and carried a Bible, a bamboo cross and a gourd of water. Not only did he preach the message of salvation, quoting from memory Bible passages dealing with salvation, he also taught them songs. And he informed them that the worship of fetishes—their form of worship for centuries—was wrong and would be punished by God.

This man, William Wade Harris, came to the Ivory Coast in 1913 and soon was considered a prophet, a miracle-worker who exorcised demons and healed the sick. Through this man, the realm of signs and wonders was opened for the people of the Ivory Coast. The power of God was undeniable, and villagers soon came to believe that the "God of Harris" was more powerful than the local "genie," or witch doctor.

Though Harris eventually was arrested by the French police and sent to Liberia (his homeland), and though the French burned all of the village chapels and ordered the converts to join the Catholic church or suffer great persecution, the effects of the "prophet" were widespread.

In the following interview, Don Young, veteran Christian

& Missionary Alliance missionary to the Ivory Coast and graduate of the Fuller School of World Mission, analyzes the effects of signs and wonders on the churches of that area today.

What is your observation of the effects of the work of the Holy Spirit in the Ivory Coast?

Young: In 1973, when Jacques Giraud came as a French evangelist to the Assemblies of God church in Abidjan, he said he didn't have the gift of healing as other evangelists might know it. However, a phenomenal development began to take place.

Since our country is sixty-six percent pagan, steeped in devil worship, a lot of people came from that sort of background. As Giraud was preaching on the uniqueness of Jesus and on the name and power of Jesus, some of these people suddenly fell to the ground. Giraud knew that this was a demon situation, and by the end of the first session many of the people were freed from demons and healed.

That was just the beginning. From the little group that came to the first meeting, the crowd grew until they couldn't hold them all in the church. They ended up going outside into the yard of the church, where there was room for several thousand. They preached there for a few nights.

There were dramatic healings, some of which happened to people in the government. One man, for example, whose leg was so paralyzed that he always had to use a cane, was healed. After several other instances of healing, word got out through government officials, the police force and the president's staff and ministers that something incredible was happening in the church in Abidjan. So the government invited us to come to a giant football stadium they had. That was in 1973.

What happened there?

Young: At that time, the stadium held around 30,000. It was filled every night for a week. They held meetings in the morning, afternoon and evening, and there were thousands of healings.

98

Since this was under the auspices of the Assemblies of God church, did other churches participate?

Young: No. That gets into political problems. Our situation was unique in that there are very few churches in each city. It's a "one mission per city" kind of thing. In Abidjan, a city of two million people, there are only twenty-two churches. Seven of them are Assemblies of God. The Christian & Missionary Alliance wasn't there at that time. So no one really cooperated, unless it was within the denomination. This made it a real movement of the people. Thousands of them were coming from everywhere at night. After several weeks of this, the president said, "I don't know what's happening here, but I want you to take whatever it is to all my major cities in the interior!"

This opened the entire center of the country to the power of God. Four crusades were held in the area in which the C&MA works—Bouake, Toumodi, Yamoussouko and Dimbokro. Crowds up to 25,000 flocked to the meetings. Many came for healings. Others came out of curiosity, hoping to see some miracle. But all heard the gospel message.

So Giraud, an Assemblies of God evangelist in France, had never seen anything like this before?

Young: No. What was happening there was a definite power encounter as the powers of God were defeating the powers of Satan. God chose an average unknown evangelist, who had seen little healing in his ministry, to manifest His power in dramatic fashion.

And practically no professing Christians were healed. It was the pagans and Muslims who were healed. And those who gave glory to God for their healing remained healed. But some returned to their idols and were again stricken with their infirmities. One man, healed of a large hernia, returned to his village to offer a sacrificed sheep to his fetish in gratitude. The moment he slit the sheep's throat, the man's hernia returned.

Finally, Giraud published the results of the "revival" in the Assemblies of God journal, *Echos Des Champs Missionnaires*, February 1974. The articles stated there had been ten months of crusades in the Ivory Coast, with 400,000 people in attendance. Approximately 68,500 Bibles and New Testaments had been given out, and people were converted in 500 different villages. Churches and chapels were built, and 15,000 people were healed from many different kinds of diseases. As evidence, 5,000 walking sticks and crutches were left at the stadiums, and about 6,000 people were baptized and incorporated into the local churches.

That was nine years ago. What is the current state of the church?

Young: It's growing in leaps and bounds. Our church went from 11,500 baptized believers to 33,500 from 1973 to 1981.

You said earlier that you referred to and employed the whole catalog of the gifts of the Spirit. Do you have any problems with students with the concept of the gifts of the Spirit being available today?

Young: There is no doubt in my mind that signs and wonders go together with church growth. It was the ministry of healing, miracles and meeting the total needs of the people that built the church in Acts, and it is still operative today.

It's interesting to note that it was a power encounter that opened our country to the gospel, and that, fifty years later, it was a power encounter that caused the church to grow.

I'm always curious when I hear evangelical preachers speak against miracles and healing for today. They have placed Christ in a time slot and really hinder His working through unbelief.

Healings and miracles have become a normal way of life to many in the Ivory Coast and His church is growing at an extraordinary pace. For this we praise His name!

South Africa

The following interview was conducted with Johan Engelbrecht, a leader from the Apostolic Faith Mission Church, the largest Pentecostal church in South Africa, and president of the Institute for Church Growth in Africa. He holds the D.Miss. degree from Fuller.

What are the implications of what God is doing through signs and wonders in Third World communities?

Engelbrecht: There is no doubt in my mind that signs and wonders are one of the major, if not *the* major, reason for church growth in South Africa. Take, for example, Richard Ngidi, a Zulu evangelist in our denomination. He's working mostly in the eastern part of the country, in Kwazulu.

Richard was just an ordinary layman, but he was very concerned about the spiritual climate of his people. So he prayed and fasted for forty days, waiting on the Lord as a layperson.

Now in that particular part of the world, fifteen years ago, there was not much emphasis on leadership training, especially among the Zulu people and other tribes. But when Richard finished this time of waiting on the Lord, the Lord clearly showed him that He wants to heal people and that He wants to touch people's lives.

Amazing things started to happen. It was nothing unusual to see the blind healed, crippled people walk, demon-possessed people delivered. I speak from firsthand knowledge because, when I pastored a church in that part of the world, I invited Richard to address the 15,000 Zulus in our area.

When he preaches, is it the "wholistic" gospel?

Engelbrecht: Yes, very much so. When he starts in an area where he was not before, and where there are nominal Christians maybe, he first pitches a tent. He then trusts God for sick people to come.

They don't advertise services over there. They don't have magazines or radio in that part of the country. So first, Richard trusts the Lord to heal a sick person. Soon the people hear about this man praying for the sick. Since they are a needy people, they come. And God starts to heal.

Usually a crusade like this takes from fourteen to twenty days. The average result is from 150 to 300 or more converts. They leave a trained pastor behind to go on with the outreach.

Now if this is not church growth in action, I wonder what church growth would ever be like. So healing plays a very important part. And Richard is not the exception.

In fact, another evangelist, Reinhard Bonnke, probably has the strongest evangelistic ministry Africa has ever seen. He is using a tent at present that holds 10,000 people. But it is too small. About three years ago he ordered a tent that will cost him the equivalent of $2 million and will hold 34,000 people. They say it will be the biggest tent ever built.

Is his ministry to the blacks or to all Africans?

Engelbrecht: Mostly to the blacks, but also to the white population. He has a team of three black ministers with him. He is a German, ordained in the Apostolic Faith Mission although he started Christ for All Nations [not related to the Dallas CFN], an evangelistic organization.

And they are seeing signs and wonders, too?

Engelbrecht: Yes. I did a research on church growth in Bophuthatswana, one of our homelands, and in Maseru, a town in Lesotho. There they pitched a 10,000-seat tent. One of Reinhard's co-workers was a young rebel he had picked up at a street meeting. He led him to the Lord, and the Lord just started to use him miraculously. I'm talking about nine years ago. His name is Kolisang, a Zulu.

Basically their approach is this. Reinhard preaches a five- to eight-minute message, then Kolisang ministers to the sick and those who want to accept the Lord.

Amazing things happen. At this particular place, when they finished, they baptized 500 converts. And again the most important reason was healing. People came and were delivered from sin—then from all kinds of sicknesses. In that part of the country, potential terrorists—sometimes even trained terrorists—would try to break up services. Then the Lord would touch them, sometimes heal them, sometimes baptize them in the Holy Spirit.

Now one of the first signs that the conversions were real would be actual truckloads of weapons, crutches and all kinds of medicines from witch doctors. They would bring these as a kind of sacrifice. Kolisang would urge them to do that, to break the power of darkness in their lives.

The second thing, I think, would be the baptism in the Holy Spirit. It would be nothing extraordinary to see 300 to 2,000 people in the front of the tent. They pray first of all to help these people accept the Lord Jesus. Secondly they pray for the sick and cast out demons, which is an integral part of their ministry. Then they pray that these people will be baptized by the Holy Spirit.

And it is not unusual to see sometimes all of them being slain in the Spirit. I don't know if you are aware of that expression. The people physically fall over, without having been touched by anyone, like a wind blowing over them.

I have on film one of their crusades in Zimbabwe. After the second night, their tent was much too small. They had to move to the soccer stadium. Thousands came. Again the team ministered healing. And the most remarkable things happened. I don't know if I should mention details, but, in general, every kind of sickness. It would be nothing extraordinary to see blind people seeing.

One particular case was a wounded ex-terrorist. He could not walk. They brought him. He was not a Christian. It was documented what actually was wrong with his spine. The Lord replaced some bones. He is now completing Bible college and the Lord is using him in a very special way.

So the miracle-working power of God is probably the foremost catalyst for church growth in South Africa?

Engelbrecht: Yes. Most of the time when they see the realness of God and the power of God, they come to the Lord and immediately experience the baptism of the Spirit.

I came from the Dutch Reformed denomination which did not believe in healing. So I was shocked when, after I accepted the Lord and started to read the Scriptures, I saw the tremendous impact healing had on the early church. I was only sixteen-and-a-half years old at that time. I was looking for the baptism of the Holy Spirit, not knowing exactly what to expect. It happened to me in a field while I was praying with a friend. And

I immediately experienced a burning desire to preach the good news and to share the reality of the Scriptures.

I was invited that particular evening to a tribal church. It's very strange for a white person to go over. In many cases you have to get a permit from the police. I stood in the service and, for the first time, gave my testimony in public. It was a Pentecostal church, and it was their custom to ask the white man to pray.

I was young, inexperienced, did not know where to lay my hands when I prayed. I figured if someone had a headache, you'd lay your hands on the head. If he had something wrong with his leg, you'd lay your hands on the leg.

When I stood there, I had no doubt that God could do anything.

A man was kneeling before me. I knew him. He was a drifter who used a lot of alcohol.

"I want to accept the Lord," he said.

I shared Christ with him and prayed for him, and he accepted the Lord. But he had a problem. He was a chronic stutterer. "You said that God can do anything. Can you pray for me?" he asked.

There I was, the first time ever in my life to pray for a sick person. Since I had figured out I should lay hands on the problem area, I asked him to push out his tongue, and I laid hands on his tongue. God touched him and healed him completely. And he became one of the most powerful evangelists in that part of the world. I preached hundreds of times with him in the next seven years. That was the start of a ministry that touched sick people. And as a result of that healing, we had to build a new big church for the people because people came to the Lord through this man.

You see, I did not have much theological training at that stage so I could not help but accept what the Word was saying. And after that, when I pastored and later had a nationwide ministry, I stressed healing.

I should just mention another very important thing. AFM started a lay movement that went on for thirty-five years and the most extraordinary healings took place. One of the catalysts in this was an American, John Lake. There is no doubt in my mind that healing, signs and wonders started this tremendous movement which not only touched southern Africa, but even went as far as the Congo, Zaire and Kenya.

DISCUSSION QUESTIONS

1. Which of the accounts given in this chapter spoke to you the most? Why? Do you believe these are dependable reports?
2. Why do you think signs and wonders are such a normal, readily accepted occurrence in other countries, yet so hesitantly accepted in our country? What would limit our ability to accept reports of signs and wonders in our churches? How can we deal with these obstacles?
3. How do you respond when it is suggested that these happenings come from a power other than that of God and the Holy Spirit? Could this be possible? Why or why not? (1 John 4:1-3; 2 Pet. 2:1-3; Eph. 4:12)
4. If we deny the possibility of signs and wonders for today, then are we also denying and/or trying to limit an aspect of God's power? What else does God's power do in our lives?
5. Have you ever experienced something that you felt was on a supernatural or "spirit" level? How did you react?
6. Do you agree with the need for "constant enduement" of God's power, as Eva Brougham speaks of? Do we need more than just being "born again" to encounter the enemy in power? Do *you* feel prepared for such an encounter?
7. How would you react to a man like William Harris? Would you accept that his "powers" were from God?

APPLICATION

Consider the following situations. Find scriptures that would help you in facing and overcoming them and then discuss what you feel your emotions and reactions would be if ever faced with one or more of them:

Demon possession; terminal illness (both in yourself and others); an encounter with someone involved in the occult; someone in a rage; temptation in the areas of alcohol, money or sex; extreme anger in yourself; someone doing things "in the name of Christ" that you know are un-Christian and against the teachings of Jesus Christ.

Can seminary professors be open to changing their ideas? Or are those ideas set in concrete? Read the firsthand accounts of how God works in some of their lives.

10

What Professors Think

compiled by Karen Ball

Fuller Theological Seminary is one of the most highly respected evangelical-oriented seminaries. Its founder, Charles E. Fuller, originator and principal speaker on "The Old-Fashioned Revival Hour," was a pioneer in the development of what today is known as the electronic church. Many notables have been and are associated with Fuller including its first president, Harold Ockenga, for more than a quarter of a century pastor of the famed Park Street Congregational Church in Boston.

What do some of the professors of the School of World Mission at Fuller Seminary think of the revolutionary approach to missiology posed by the course MC510, Signs, Wonders and Church Growth?

Their evaluations, along with reactions from students, provide another basis for considering this highly important subject.

Dean S. Gilliland

For Dean S. Gilliland, professor of contextualization of theology at the school and a former missionary to Nigeria (where he was president of a seminary), the offering of the class came as no surprise.

He explained that Peter Wagner, an expert on church growth and a professor at Fuller, had become convinced that if something appears in the Scriptures, then Christians today ought to be seeing it. Wagner maintained that the churches which were manifesting the signs and wonders were often the growing churches.

"What we saw as a faculty, in the beginning," Gilliland said, "was that we should offer this as a course because we ought to be open to the Holy Spirit. If there is something that the Spirit should be teaching the churches today, we here at the School of World Mission don't want to resist."

Gilliland felt that Wagner basically was supporting the fact that God is doing something in certain churches today, and that those churches are growing. "So if it became a matter of looking into this thing historically and standing against the generally held theory that miracles and healing were only for the apostolic church, then we would be willing to make that stand."

All of the faculty of the School of World Mission have served as missionaries. According to Gilliland, they have experienced the environment of spirits and the spirit world. Because of this, there were no objections raised when the class was suggested, even though several faculty members wisely warned against excesses.

Equipping American Missionaries

"We need to prepare and equip typical Western, American-oriented students, who have an American worldview, for the mission field. We must help them better understand the things that are being seen on the mission field. Things which they have been unable either to interpret, accept or utilize."

Reactions of the students to the class have ranged from "good to almost ecstatic," Gilliland says. "Very rarely do we have courses with that much affirmation. And I think I would be in a position to hear the negative opinions, because I don't have any personal involvement in the course. Students do talk to me a lot."

Students who have taken the course are from many different cultures and backgrounds. And they don't have to participate in the "practical session" where the prayer and healing experiences are practiced, if they don't want to.

"When I visited the course, Professor Wimber gave everyone

an opportunity to leave before they entered into that practical session. I was not aware of anyone leaving.''

Gilliland anticipates that the class will be continued. ''We've given it our largest classroom, and there are always more there than those that have signed up for the course. And each class is evaluated by the students. I think this one will come off with high marks. When you see people being prayed for and receiving healing and other manifestations of the Spirit every week, you know it's pretty hard not to evaluate a course highly.''

Gilliland comes from a Methodist background where he was brought up in a ''strict holiness tradition where manifestations of the Spirit, laying on of hands, divine healing as an 'every Sunday sort of thing' were quite far out, an almost unacceptable feature of teaching and experiencing the Holy Spirit.''

Gilliland attended two of the nine class sessions and admits that he has had to relearn some things.

''I've got certain 'gut reactions' that have been programmed into my mind and into my whole theological makeup from the time I was a young person. But I agree with my colleagues totally that if God is using a particular means—and if the church is multiplying through that—then we better be on the side of that, rather than against it.''

Charles H. Kraft

Charles H. Kraft is professor of intercultural communications and African studies, a former missionary to Nigeria and a graduate of Wheaton College. He is the only professor other than Wimber and Wagner who actually attended the whole course. He believes that people, to be adequately trained for the mission field, must be taught to deal with healings as a part of the spiritual message, because ''that's where the rest of the world is.''

''My experience in Nigeria,'' Kraft explained, ''was that the people had difficulty understanding preachers who didn't heal, and healers who didn't preach. These people perceived the works of healing as coming from divine power rather than from impersonal medicine.''

Kraft maintains that to separate preaching and healing is to perpetuate the mission philosophy of a century ago: Civilize to evangelize.

"We've been Westernizing first, then trying to convert them to a supernaturalistic Christian point-of-view within their Westernization. It results, very often, in quite a superficial kind of nominal Christianity," he says.

One of the reasons for this separation, according to Kraft, is that evangelicalism has been striving for respectability in the American scene. To achieve this, the move has been toward an artificial academic respectability. For Kraft, such a move is one out of the real world into an intellectual world. People move away from the things that are emotional, things that are behavior-oriented and practice-oriented, into things that are more school-information, intellect-oriented. That, to Kraft, results in a real problem.

"At one end of the spectrum are those who are desperate enough to try anything. At the other end are those who are secure enough to experiment. It's the ones in the middle, who are trying to move toward greater respectability, that very often are insecure about trying something that is quite novel. And I think that's where most evangelicalism, as I have experienced it anyway, fits."

Many of these evangelicals, in Kraft's opinion, come from fundamentalist, conservative backgrounds which promote dispensationalism and the kind of reformed theology seen in Benjamin Warfield.

"We are taught that miracles and healing are not part of our experience. Such things ended in the first century, and we'll never experience them. From this background we go to conservative colleges, then to the mission field. There we find that, very often, God is doing these things. Dreams, healings, demon-possession, all are experienced. So, to keep our belief system intact, we explain away all of these things. Soon the people just stop telling us about the happenings. They know we aren't open to them."

Anthropological Openness

Kraft went through a change in his attitude as he worked on

an undergraduate degree in anthropology. He developed an "anthropological openness" to balance his "theological closedness." For a while, the two views caused struggles. Then Kraft realized that Nigerians were sharing more with him because he was not totally closed to accepting the things that were taking place in their lives.

"So I just began to open myself up to some of these things. And I have been saying for several years that we need to get into this dimension. So when the opportunity came to us to offer this course, I was one of its strongest advocates. And I said, 'When that is offered, I'm going to be there.' "

His evaluation of the course after taking it: "It was super. And while some of the stories of healings won't hold up," he said, "the ones that do will aid in documentation and research in the area of signs and wonders.

"John Wimber," Kraft said, "takes an analytical approach to what he is doing. He is very impressive in the way he can pray for healing and analyze what he is doing and what's going on with the person who is being healed. That's what makes it so neat when we actually see a healing take place. We are led into the analytical process, then we see what has been analyzed actually happening.

"Also, Wimber has been able to encourage others in the gift of what he calls 'the word of knowledge.' Students become able to stand and state a specific need of someone else within the gathering. Then the students do the praying for that need."

Kraft also is confident that the class will be continued. He believes that, although there may be some objection to it, Fuller Seminary has the necessary degree of security in its position as a "pioneer" in relation to the whole of theological education.

"We know that with our administration, we are free to be creative and innovative, as long as we are responsible about it."

"I don't believe that miracles ever have been absent from our culture. I think our eyes have been clouded over so that we haven't seen things. When people open themselves up to more of the miraculous, I feel that God gives it to them."

And he has more to learn, Kraft says.

"Wouldn't it be stupid just to sit here in an 'ivory tower' and assume that I know it all and that this student, just because he has a different color of skin, doesn't know anything. Yet he has the intelligence to believe that God is going to heal, while I strain and say something like 'Your will be done.' It's been a fascinating experience. I would hate to be so closed that I missed it."

Glenn Barker

The late Glenn Barker, provost of the seminary, approved the introduction of the course because he felt that the charismatic movement in the world has demonstrated that "God is in it."

"Three out of every four Christians in Latin America are charismatics," Barker says. "Those churches which have been most open to the ministry of the Holy Spirit also have appeared to be receiving the greatest blessings. That being true, and since our school exists for research purposes as to how the mission of Christ should be conducted, it became apparent that this was an area in which we needed to have a better understanding. We knew it needed to be approached within the care and protection of a theological seminary where anthropologists, sociologists and psychologists could research all the possibilities present."

Barker believes that where the ministry of the Spirit is present in a powerful way, there is a clear understanding and grasp of the ordination of the individual Christian for ministry. He explains that churches got away from the manifestations of the Spirit because of people called "the enthusiasts."

"These were people who depended upon their emotional experience with the Spirit of God and felt that they could say or do anything. They lacked the commitment to the biblical truth of weighing and testing everything by the Word of God. As a result, the church came to look upon them with trepidation and suspicion.

"Then came the teaching that the age of miracles and the work of the Holy Spirit was limited to the Apostolic Age. Of course, no biblical texts say this, but that became part of the explanation of mainline Protestants that these things, these special expressions of the presence of the Spirit, were more likely satanic counterfeits. So many were taught to be fearful of these movements.''

A major change came, according to Barker, when fine, disciplined biblical scholars within the movement began to test everything by the Word of God. These scholars are trained theologically and are trying to give a more appropriate support for the gifts.

"Karl Barth himself recognized that, in the history of the church, two areas of theology had never really been well developed," Barker says. "One was ecclesiology (doctrine of the church); the other was the doctrine of the Spirit. Barth felt that this was the next major area where the church would need to commit itself in its thinking.

Testing All Things

"We need to test all things," Barker explains. "This is a time when churches are not totally comfortable, not totally sure as to what all 'signs and wonders' really mean. But there are times when, even beyond our understanding, we commit ourselves to obedience to the Spirit. We don't always have to understand everything we do. Yet everything must be tested by the Word of God.''

Barker also believes it would be tragic if, in the name and power of God, the people of God should be divided. "I do not believe that God is a God of division among His people. And we are very concerned that all ministries function in such a way that there is always the unity of the body of Christ which has been both celebrated and experienced. That is why one must be cautious.

"I don't think we should ever, in any of these things, move without careful theological undergirding. Especially as teachers, we must be sure that what we say is validated. In the very nature of what it means to teach others is the need to teach them according to the Word of God.''

Barker also feels that it is their responsibility, as a leadership-oriented seminary, to do what they believe in, what they feel should be done.

"For some reason," Barker says, "Fuller has been a seminary close to the edge of missions from the very beginning. It's lived out there, and that's always made us more vulnerable to misunderstanding.

"Of course, it also is a temptation to become arrogant; to over trust ourselves, whereas we want to be in total obedience to God. But it always is distressing if, in our obedience, we create an obstacle to somebody else's faith or belief. That is, for me, a very difficult tension. We live within that tension of being obedient to God and also being responsible to the people of God. We belong to the church. We're not here for ourselves."

KAREN BALL *is a professional Christian journalist.*

DISCUSSION QUESTIONS

1. What did the overall reaction of these theologians to the course seem to be?
2. What is your reaction to the "Civilize to Evangelize" philosophy? How does this philosophy correlate to the manner in which Christ performed His ministry?
3. At what area of the spectrum mentioned by Charles Kraft are you? Why?
4. How do you feel about analyzing a healing? Is it possible to be over emotional or go overboard in an area such as signs and wonders? How can we, as Christians, avoid this? (2 Tim. 4:2-5; Phil. 2:1-4,12,13).
5. Have you ever seen or experienced a division in fellowship because of disagreement over doctrine or theology? Can Christians ensure that this doesn't happen when considering signs and wonders? How? (John 15:1-8; 2 Tim. 2:14-16,22-26)

APPLICATION

Consider the last paragraph of the article. Discuss how this applies not only to the church, but to each of us as individual followers of Christ. How can we learn to balance the aspects of the "difficult tension" Glenn Barker speaks of?

In the previous chapter Charles Kraft described his early impressions of MC510. Now he brings us up to date on his thinking and ministry five years later.

11

Five Years Later

by Charles H. Kraft

I am one of the many whose lives have been profoundly affected as a result of the decision of the SWM faculty to offer the MC510 course. My wife and I attended every session.

Ours were fairly typical evangelical backgrounds. We were brought up in evangelical churches in which the authority of the Bible, the plight of the lost, the need for salvation through faith in Christ and the like were strongly asserted. But out and out miracles were neither expected nor did they happen.

We met at Wheaton College, attended Ashland (Ohio) Seminary, studied missions for a year at the Kennedy School of Missions and in 1957 headed for Nigeria to serve as pioneer church and language/Bible translation missionaries under the Brethren Church (Ashland, Ohio). We went out well-trained in biblical studies, anthropology and linguistics.

It wasn't long, however, before a deficiency in our training turned up. In a conversation with several Nigerian leaders, I asked what they saw as the greatest problem of the Nigerian people. Without hesitation, they cited the problem of evil spirits. These spirits, they told me, cause such things as disease, accidents and death, hinder fertility of people, animals and fields, bring bad weather, destroy relationships, harass the innocent and so on. But I had nothing to suggest except that they take the matter to God.

Though my anthropological training had enabled me to be both more observant and more open to Nigerian life, neither that nor my biblical and theological training had provided me with any constructive approaches in what was the most important area of their life. By the grace of God, people responded to Christ in significant numbers anyway. But by and large, though, they retained their pre-Christian practices with regard to spiritual power since neither they nor we their missionaries knew there was another option within Christianity.

The frustration of this part of my Nigerian experience lingered in my memory as I completed graduate school, taught at two secular universities and eventually became a part of the Fuller faculty (in 1969). In this position, then, I began to receive two other nudges in the direction of openness to learning MC510. First, as we discussed the church worldwide, it became obvious that the most rapid growth was taking place among those with a Pentecostal or charismatic orientation. Secondly, as our student body grew, more and more Pentecostals and charismatics came to Fuller and I began to trust them.

Additionally, I had gotten to know John Wimber who became the "credible witness" used of God in my conversion to this dimension of Christianity. We on the SWM faculty knew and respected John as a church growth analyst before he got into a healing ministry.

The Course—My Paradigm Shift

Then came January 1982. There were over eighty students in class each Monday evening in the MC510 course. I as a senior professor was very visible so I wanted to move cautiously. Yet the perspective was so convincing and compatible with the direction in which I was groping that I soon lost my reserve—so much so that by about the fourth session, John asked me to do the lecture on worldview, focusing on the shift that was taking place in my own experience.

The struggle for me was not mainly intellectual. I had long since abandoned my early dispensationalist training and come to see Jesus as "the same yesterday, today and forever" (Heb. 13:8). If He is the same, I expected miracles today as well as yesterday. It is just that, to this point, I could not recall ever having seen something I could confidently and unambiguously call a miracle. The course provided opportunities to see, thus confirming and filling out my thinking.

The "words of knowledge" were a bigger intellectual challenge. I had in my writing already departed from the standard evangelical position by concluding that a living God is still a revealing God (*Christianity in Culture*, pp. 207,237). But I had never seen it happen so clearly. So these contemporary revelations filled an experience gap that I had already allowed for.

The greatest challenge was, however, to my own Christian practice. For we were taught 1) that we are all to minister healing to others and 2) that we should take advantage of this class setting to begin practicing such a ministry. This was scary! I would literally ask God not to let anyone near me stand up to be prayed for! I was afraid it wouldn't work if I was involved. Maybe I didn't "have the gift" or, worse yet, was too sinful for God to use me in this way. Sometimes when someone near me did stand, I would back off to watch the students deal with the situation. Perhaps, I reasoned, the students would think I really did know how to pray for people and was simply giving them a chance!

Seeing people healed was, however, so exciting I couldn't stop talking about it. This led others to assume I knew how to pray for them, which I did whenever I couldn't get out of it. But not much tangible seemed to happen from 1982 to 1983. I was, however, moving in the direction of greater involvement, having my change of attitude (my "paradigm shift") confirmed and moving closer to what I call my "practice shift."

My Practice Shift

I had shared my stories with the pastor of the church I belong to (Pasadena Covenant Church). In early 1984, then, he announced that our evening services would be changed to a "praise and worship" format with an invitation to people to stay after to "pray for specific needs." He asked me to be in charge of the prayer room. Though people did not come in large

117

numbers, I did get to pray with someone nearly every week. This gave me some practice and enough happened to give me more confidence. I also began to be invited by various Sunday school classes to teach on healing. Sometimes this resulted in opportunities to demonstrate what I was talking about in front of the class.

Other pivotal events in this transition period were 1) the straightening out of a sin in my life; 2) receiving an encouraging prophecy through a person who had no idea what he was referring to; 3) the symptoms of blockage in some of the blood vessels near my heart gone after prayer; and 4) a weekend retreat during which two people I prayed for were healed, one quite dramatically.

These experiences brought me to the point where I said to the Lord, "I don't care if You embarrass me. I'm going to pray for anyone who wants to be prayed for. I'm going to be active rather than passive in praying for healing." This was my "practice shift."

With this approach I have by now experienced many good things, both in the United States and abroad. I haven't seen any blind gain their sight or any crippled people jump up and walk—yet. But God has used me to minister healing to many with other physical problems and to many with spiritual and emotional ills.

Some of What I've Been Learning

There are several aspects of this experience that have become very important to me. What follows is a summary of some of the more important things He has been teaching me:

1. The real issue is *ministry, not simply healing*. It is easy for us to focus on the spectacular—a leg lengthened, cancer gone. But these are but parts of and incidental to God's main purpose—that someone minister to hurting ones whom He loves. Before we seek to take authority over someone's physical, psychological or spiritual problem, our prayer is that God will do whatever He wants to do, no matter what we may ask. He may do what we ask or

something quite different. And He may do whatever He does either immediately or over a series of ministry sessions. But He wants to minister and always will do something if we will but become active as His agents.

2. Seeing this as ministry is *especially important for those whom God does not heal*. It is easy for someone whom God heals to feel ministered to. But what about the one who is not healed? Many for whom I pray do not seem to get relief from the problem they were most concerned about, though often they go away blessed because God has obviously dealt with something else. But for those who seem to receive no help there are several important principles: 1) we do not know why God heals when He heals and why He does not when He seems not to, nor 2) do we have the right to command God to do what we think He ought to do. If a person is not healed, therefore, 3) we have no right to add to the person's woes by blaming him/her for a lack of faith or sin in his/her life. Though we know that such things may cause blockage and may, therefore, lovingly ask the person to examine him/herself, we cannot state for sure what the problem is in any given case. 4) Ministering to a person must be done lovingly if it is to be genuinely Christian and to mediate healing.

3. I believe that, though we often use the word "prayer" when speaking about this kind of ministry, there is a *difference between praying and taking authority*. Jesus gave the disciples "power and authority to drive out all demons and to cure diseases" (Luke 9:1). He modeled this when "he ordered the fever to leave" (Luke 4:39) and when He said to the leper "be clean" (Luke 5:13). He expected the disciples to use their authority to feed the 5,000 (Luke 9:13) and, I think, to still the storm when He was asleep in the boat (Luke 8:25). Important transactions take place in the spiritual realm when we take this delegated authority or when we use it to bless or to curse, to forgive or to refuse forgiveness (John 20:23).

There is, of course, an important place for prayer.

Nothing gets done without it. But prayer is primarily preparation for ministry. In prayer we assure both God and ourselves that we desire His will, not ours; we ask for God to minister to the person who seeks His help; we confess any sin and ask for His power to defeat the enemy in the coming encounter. Without prayer we have no authority and power. But in the encounter itself, we are to take the authority given us by Jesus and in His name *command* the problem to be resolved. At this point we are working as His agents, with His full authority to rearrange things in the spiritual realm.

4. What about the *"success rate"*? As noted, not everyone gets healed of the problem to which I address myself. Perhaps in the physical area my average is around fifty percent. I think it is higher in dealing with spiritual problems, though that is harder to estimate. It appears, however, that nearly all receive some sort of tangible blessing from God.

5. One of the things that has surprised me is the amount of *learning and experimenting* involved in a healing ministry. I had assumed that people received the "gift" all at once. What I experience is a gradual learning process that comes along with constant practice and a lot of risk taking. The learning seems to center in at least three areas: 1) ministering to people, 2) listening to God and 3) developing greater faith and confidence to risk doing what one thinks one hears from God. The fear of being wrong is a powerful impediment, but God seems to bless more when we launch out in faith in spite of our fear, and then when we make mistakes, pick ourselves up and try again.

6. Praying for healing is *not a matter of gifting but of obedience*. The disciples were empowered and commanded to minister in this way (Luke 9:1,2) and later told to teach everything they had been taught (Matt. 28:20). But not everyone seems to be equally effective with all types of problems. I have noted, for example, that to date God seems to give me most success in the physical area with

problems related to the bony structures of the body. But even more than physical problems, God seems to use me in discerning and ministering in spiritual and psychological areas, especially those that involve the interference of minor spirits. I have seldom had a word of knowledge concerning a physical problem. But as I minister, God usually gives me multiple words concerning a person's spiritual and psychological needs. Could it be that I have more faith for these problems? Or has God gifted me more in one area than another?

7. This ministry is to *persons as wholes*. Any attempt to divide persons into physical, psychological and spiritual beings in a healing ministry is pointless. We minister to the whole person, no matter what the problem that brought him/her. People who come to me with physical problems often need ministry in psychological and/or spiritual areas. Sometimes God chooses to deal with that problem in place of the physical problem. Sometimes, however, the physical healing is given as soon as that other problem is dealt with. I have seen arms, shoulders and legs "automatically" corrected when a spirit was sent away.

8. Overall, God is teaching me such things as: 1) that I need to attempt to minister healing even though frightened and skeptical; 2) that God often blesses even such weak attempts; 3) that "even I" can be used of God in such a ministry; 4) that God shows things through words of knowledge; 5) that the "success" rate increases with practice; 6) that both healing and "faithing" are learned through experience; 7) that God richly blesses the one who prays as well as the one prayed for; 8) that even when the person prayed for is not healed, God often ministers to him/her; 9) that even after much experience there is still much to learn; and 10) that even after seeing God do numerous exciting things, one may still find him/herself skeptical from time to time!

Concluding Remarks

The MC510 course has led me into the most earthshaking

experience of my Christian life. I have been a Christian now for forty-two years. My Christian life has been very satisfying and rewarding, but I never dreamed it could be so good! I feel as if I have moved to an entirely new plane on which all of the things I have believed for these many years have taken on new life.

I find myself reading the Bible with new eyes—knowing that miracles and deliverances and revelations from God and angels and demons and all those things I used to read about only as inspired history are for us today! I find a new desire to pray, to talk to God and to listen to Him. I experience a new boldness in speaking about my faith, a new confidence that God is in fact who I have long believed Him to be. There is new power and authority in ministry, as well as a compelling desire to minister to others. The fruit of the Spirit (Gal. 5:22,23) is easier to practice. Tears of compassion are frequently in my eyes.

I am (as my wife can testify) still pitifully human. But there are enough changes that it seems clear that nothing short of the power of God is at work in me. And I like it a lot!

Could this be what the kingdom is intended to be? I believe God expects us to see with kingdom eyes, to live as kingdom people, to minister with kingdom power and authority. When we do, I believe we experience a new level of normalcy—what I like to call "kingdom normalcy." In the kingdom of God, things we refer to as miracles are the order of the day.

I like the "new" normalcy so much I never want to go back to the old.

DISCUSSION QUESTIONS

1. Kraft says that many Nigerian converts retained their pre-Christian practices with regard to spiritual power. What do you think this means? How could it affect the Christian life in Nigeria?
2. Could it be possible that an African Christian could consult a witch doctor and still remain a Christian? Or would they lose their salvation?

3. Discuss why there was a time lag between Kraft's accepting the idea of miraculous healing and beginning to practice it. Have you had similar experiences?
4. Is praying for the sick done just by those with the gift of healing or by every Christian? How are those with the gift of healing any different from those who do not have it?

APPLICATION

Go through the ten items in Kraft's point number eight. These are excellent guidelines for those who pray for the sick. Begin to pray for some who are sick specifically attempting to follow those principles.

For some of the students the MC510 course was life-changing. For others it raised questions they are still wrestling with. Join students from different walks of life as they relate their personal experiences and impressions.

12

The Students' View

compiled by Karen Ball

The lecture is over. The largest lecture room at the seminary is crowded to the walls with students sitting on the floor. Some stand to stretch, but few move for fear of losing their seats. The teacher, a large rotund man with a lion-like appearance—thick bushy hair, beard and moustache—observes the class with thoughtful eyes. In a calm voice, one easily given to humor, he states that those who wish to leave before the "practical" session of the class may do so. No one does. He nods slightly, then proceeds.

"Are there any words of knowledge tonight?" he asks.

There is a pause. Then a young woman stands to tell of an image she had of someone's back. Near the waist on the right-hand side, there appears to be a disc, an "oval shape which seems to have an intense light coming from it. It seems to be reflecting off something metallic."

At this point, another woman stands and exclaims that it is she who is experiencing the back pain, in that exact area...and she is wearing a metal back brace.

This is not a demonstration of magic. Nor is it a hoax. The event is the class, "Signs, Wonders and Church Growth," which began meeting at Fuller Seminary in 1982. Students who took the first course were interviewed as to their reactions and opinions of the contents, the method and the teacher.

The First Word of Knowledge

Nancy Tribley, one of the students, came from a widely divergent theological background. She was originally an Episcopalian, then United Presbyterian, and now was attending the area Foursquare Church. She had been accepted as a missionary candidate in Japan under the Language Institute for Evangelism when she heard about Wimber's course.

When asked if she had made any theological transitions because of the course she replied that she and her husband were both charismatics "in the sense that I speak in tongues in prayer. But as far as doing anything like healing...I made a definite transition in this area.

"I feel that it helped firm up my theology," she explained, "at least as far as healing goes. And this course has given me a chance to be receptive to just trying to find out if I was having a word of knowledge or something like that. I am able to be open to that and not feel embarrassed. When I had my first word of knowledge, or what I thought might be one, I was able to say it and just see what happened because of the receptive atmosphere of the class. And it was a valid word of knowledge about a girl with a back problem."

Nancy said the only change she would make in the class would be to schedule more time actually to "see others healing and doing it yourself." When asked if she had found opportunities to use the gifts, she said yes. She had received a word of knowledge in each subsequent class following her first experience with this gift.

"And I will very definitely continue to exercise the gifts. Both my husband and I will do so wherever we can find the opportunity. I find myself looking more and being willing to ask someone who is sick if I may pray for him or her. I have been able to do that even at work, where I would never have felt comfortable doing it before."

She also commented on the popularity of the class. "Most classes at Fuller start out with everyone there, but by the tenth week the attendance kind of dribbles down. You've got a lot of people thinking, 'I've got papers to do, and I can get the notes from someone else.' But in this class, there have probably been more people there each week.

"It's as John Wimber says, we're dealing with a dynamic. It's not just the Word of God; it's the living Word of God. And the dynamic demands expression. If we just respond to that demand, then the theology will catch up with us somewhere along the line."

Casting Out Demons

Marge Dayton, a marriage counselor and graduate of Fuller Seminary, took the course because "there are always things in the field of counseling that puzzle one. We have been going on theories and new breakthroughs for years, and you just want to get better educated."

Since she had never been introduced to the ideas and concepts of Wimber's class before, she came in with "pre-learned theological concepts" that did not encourage really "expecting anything to happen when you prayed for healing."

"This course, and what I've seen and done here, has increased my faith. I've had a nagging disc problem for a year and a half. It's been prayed for before, but this time when they prayed for me there was a real difference. I felt a great deal of heat up and down my back, and a kind of massaging up and down my neck and the back of my legs."

When asked about the strengths of the course, Marge replied that she believes that it is "ministering to the whole person. And it's done very well from a psychological standpoint. There was no guilt heaped on people. There was a ring of authenticity that I have not seen before. And I feel that the things I have learned here will be useful to me in the area of counseling. Especially since there are so many today who are involved in the occult. Because of this class I won't ever be afraid of that type of thing again.

"I have had people come in for counseling who had very bad manifestations of demons. There was one case where the girlfriend was telling me about her boyfriend. They were looking for a counselor for him, a counselor who had 'heavy duty' training. As we talked, I began to see that perhaps he was experiencing some demon oppression, and I asked the girl what she thought of that. She said that another pastor also had thought this might be true. And her boyfriend was thinking that it could be true, too.

"So I called John Wimber. We arranged to see this man at my house. We prayed for him, and John used Scripture, commanding the demon to leave the man's body.

"Finally, after several demons left, the man said he felt 'greatly relieved.' He came to see me two weeks later, and I learned that this demon oppression had first happened to him as a small boy. Apparently his family had been involved in the occult. He was still having some psychological problems, but the evil manifestations were gone. That was encouraging.

"We just need to believe that greater is He that is in us, than he that is in the world."

"I Laid Hands on My Father"

Jim Walker, a freshman at Fuller, attended the class along with his wife. When asked why, Walker replied, "The evidence is plain. Signs and wonders are there to be seen. This has been a part of my background. But I wanted to know more about it."

Walker came from a Quaker family; his wife was from the Church of God.

The class, he said, had been "really remarkable. Being able to hear people say that they can see an evil spirit oppressing someone, then breaking the power of that spirit. Then seeing the person after they had been healed...."

Since Walker is planning to be a minister, he was asked what his plans were. "I would like to go back to Wyoming and plant a church there. I have an idea forming in my mind to incorporate a signs, wonders and healing ministry in the center of a church where God can really be free to move in whatever way He wants, and use His loving, healing power to confirm His goodness to His people. This affirms for us that God is a good God, that He loves and cares."

Walker also shared an experience that he had had with his father. "I went up to Wyoming for a weekend of snowmobiling. I knew that my father would be there, and I knew that he had been sick, but I didn't realize how bad he was. He had some back problems, but there was also some very bad pain in his abdomen. And there was some concern about his heart. He overworks himself and doesn't really get the sleep he should. I think the stress created by this situation caused the suffering.

"The week before I went up to the meeting, I kept thinking about him, and I believe that God was preparing me to minister to him. I felt that it would be wonderful to go up there and pray for him to be healed.

"What happened was, during a service that our church group was having there, I felt sick and had to go back to my room. My father was there, and he was feeling terrible. I began telling him about the class at Fuller, and how God really does heal people. He was hurting so bad that after about an hour, he just knelt down in the motel room and said, 'Pray for me now.' So I prayed.

"I laid my hands on his back, and he said that it got real warm, and the pain left immediately. He had been struggling with this pain for two months. But there was still pain in his abdomen, so my wife, who was there also, joined me in prayer. Then she seemed to catch a little flash of insight. 'I see guilt written all over your face,' she said to my father. 'You feel guilty because you have abused your body, and you can't receive God's goodness because you don't think you deserve it.'

"So we prayed with him, and he confessed this to God. He was praying and crying. It is unique to pray with your father like that. After awhile I asked him if he was healed, and he started crying again and said yes. The pain had left him just a moment before I asked. I told him how much I loved him, and it was a very affirming time. It's been four weeks now, and he has had no more problems with the pain, and I don't believe he will."

Fuller Is a Different Culture

For Elaine Stewart, the subjects covered and experienced in the class were a normal and natural part of faith. A freshman from Charlotte, North Carolina, she was raised in a Pentecostal church where "this sort of thing is the norm. It's nothing unusual for us to experience the moving of the Spirit in our services."

When asked why she attended the class, Elaine answered that she was interested in finding out how other denominations experienced the presence of the Lord and how they accepted it.

"I wanted to see how the Lord was moving in other people's lives in other denominations. And I have seen that now. It's thrilling to see how they accept it!"

She told of instances in Wimber's class when those who were new to "this kind of thing" would gather in groups during the practical session of the class. "There was a couple there, and the wife had an ear infection. At first they seemed a little apprehensive. But the woman said she was willing to be open to whatever God wanted for her. We students laid our hands on her and prayed. She didn't know what to think at first, but then she got excited. She said she felt a warm sensation, and her earache was gradually disappearing. She also had a lump in her throat from infection, and it just dissolved.

"Since then I have watched her grow spiritually. She has told how she would go out and pray for other people. She said that this was becoming a norm in her life."

Coming to Fuller was a big step for Elaine. "The culture here is very different. I've had a big learning experience, not just in the class but otherwise too. But I felt that in this class, those who were really interested in healing and manifestations of the Spirit would experience the feeling of the presence of the Lord working in their lives.

"I've always felt that if you were going to walk with the Lord you have to do so daily. You could go by just head knowledge, but I like both head knowledge and heart knowledge."

Just prior to starting the class with Wimber, Elaine was healed of allergies. She had been taking shots for four years and was restricted in what she could eat. "But God completely healed me, and that's a miracle.

"With this class," she said, "I also wanted to feel the nearness of fellowship with Christians. I hoped that I would have contact with people who really wanted more of the Spirit of the Lord in their lives. And that's what happened. You really feel a closeness to them.''

Some Lingering Doubts

Of course, not all reactions have been 100 percent positive. Ole Oystese, a visiting Scandinavian scholar with a strong Lutheran background, listed questions he felt needed to be answered.

''The course on signs, wonders and church growth has put to fire in me a long-smouldering spark—a desire to be able to minister to my people with greater spiritual authority,'' he said.

''In spite of this, I have not been able to suppress a feeling of uncertainty and fear. Being conscious of how hazardous it may be to put the power of the almighty God in the hands of sinful man, I would like to call your attention to some questions which, according to my understanding, should be studied before signs and wonders are made the central core of church work.''

Oystese then asked:

What does Matthew 4:1-11 mean as far as our ministry with signs and wonders goes? Did not Satan try to teach Jesus a way to accomplish effective ''church growth''? Why did he continually come back with the same temptation: to make Jesus reveal the glory, the power and the omnipotence of God instead of His weakness and His foolishness, to make Jesus a wonder-maker, to make Him escape pain and be vigorous, resourceful and strong (Matt. 8:31-33; John 7:3-9, 6:14; Matt. 27:42-44)?

Why did Jesus so often tell healed people not to make Him known as a wondermaker?

Does John 6:26 mean that signs and wonders may create delusive effects when they are put in the center of our ministry?

May the effectiveness of using signs and wonders for church growth come from the fact that everybody likes bread, likes to escape suffering and pain, likes power and resourcefulness, but not to the same degree appreciate the foolishness of the cross?

May the multitude in churches that have given signs and wonders a central place in their work be the same multitude that wanted to make "Jesus the breadmaker" their king (John 6:14)?

May we in making signs and wonders the main part of our ministry be like Moses asking to see the glory of God (Ex. 33)? Why does God find it necessary to conceal His glory and reveal Himself in weakness? Why not reveal His glorious face and not just His back?

Is it unbelief to leave it to God to decide what kind of answer will best help the sick one and the kingdom of God? Such a prayer will, of course, be ineffective in the case of "faith healing." But why should it be so if God is the healer, and if faith is trust in His wisdom and not in the wisdom of my proposal?

It seems that there must be a difference between *asking* God for help and *dictating* to Him to heal. There must be room—even in the prayer for healing—for a humble "not as I will...."

What can we learn from the "but if not" in Daniel 3:18?

What does it mean that wonders are "signs"? What do they signify?

What does it mean to be saved "in the hope"?

What does Peter mean by arguing that salvation is "kept in heaven ready to be revealed in the last days and that we now "for a while...may have to suffer" (1 Pet. 1)?

What is the difference between the "theologia gloriae" and the "theologia crucis," as far as our ministry to the sick is concerned?

What does Jesus mean by saying that those are the blessed ones that do not see, but do believe?

"I am not sure I have the right answer to these questions," Oystese concluded. "Wimber and others seem to be effective both in church growth and in their healing ministry. I would not be honest if I said: So am I! Nevertheless, these are some of the questions which, according to my understanding, should be taken seriously before we rush into the healing ministry."

The Reality of God in Action

Nancy McRae is the secretary to the dean of the School of World Mission at Fuller, as well as the school receptionist. She took the class after seeing how popular it was at registration.

"It's wall-to-wall people each week," she said. "I think the excitement over the course comes from seeing the reality of God in action."

On the first night of the class, Nancy was sick with the flu. She had planned just to register, then go home since she knew the session was being taped. But a friend said, "If you're ill, this isn't the class to miss." Nancy attended, and Wimber, through a word of knowledge, described her illness, telling her what kind of flu she had and recounting a stomach problem.

"He also pointed out that I had experienced quite a bit of apprehension about what was going on, which was true because it was new to me. I came into the course not really expecting God to work in my presence. Although I had prayed for people who were sick, it wasn't with the anticipation that He was really going to do something. So when John Wimber prayed for me that night, he told me that God had given him a message for me. Because of my lack of groundwork for faith in the healing, God said I would experience a spiritual battle.

" 'I believe you will be healed by tomorrow morning,' Wimber told me. 'But the symptoms will come back and you'll need to hang on by faith for this healing.'

"And that's exactly what happened. I felt great the next morning, then experienced a relapse. But the Lord gave me some special verses all week as I read the Bible in my quiet times. By the next class my symptoms were ninety-five percent gone, and I hadn't had to miss any work."

Responding to Wimber's challenge to the class to get out and pray for people, Nancy found herself in several circumstances where she began to exercise her gifts. She found one friend sick in bed with a migraine when she went to visit her. After asking if it was all right, Nancy prayed for her healing. When she checked on her friend the next day, she found that the pain was not totally gone.

"We learned in class that if the pain doesn't all go away, we pray again. This time my friend's son, who is mentally retarded but full of faith and love for the Lord, joined me in the prayer. We both put our hands on her head, and I heard her son praying, 'Oh Lord, You can do anything.' We felt the heat on her head, which is one of the signs that the Lord is actively healing, so I was sure she had been taken care of. Sure enough, she was soon bright-eyed and feeling great. That was my first experience of seeing God answer like that.''

Nancy has a Presbyterian background but currently attends a Congregational church. "I come from a good solid evangelical background," she stated, "where there was always the idea that we prayed for the people who were sick. But we never did so with the expectancy that God was really going to heal them. Now the Lord is using me, and it's so thrilling because it is a whole new avenue of ministry. It's been great.''

DISCUSSION QUESTIONS

1. If you have ever experienced a manifestation of a gift of the Spirit, can you remember how you felt the first time? If you haven't experienced this, how do you think you would react?

2. Why do you think this class was so popular? Would you have taken it, and would you have participated in both the lecture and practical sessions? Why or why not?

3. Do you believe that the things studied and learned in MC510 are things you would be able to use in day-to-day situations or even at work (that is, Marge Dayton, the counselor)? How do you think your friends and co-workers would react?

4. Have you ever been made to feel guilty about some aspect of Christianity? What was your reaction? Why would this be especially detrimental in a teaching situation? (Prov. 3:1-13; Luke 17:1,2)

5. Are there aspects of your faith that you have just accepted without understanding why you do them (that is, baptism, communion and so forth)? Why is it important to understand the background and reasons for what you do in faith and worship?

6. Consider the questions that Oystese raised. Do you

have any similar questions?

APPLICATION

Once again, compare the "pros and cons" of signs and wonders for yourself, both as an individual and as a group.

1. Do you believe that you have a good understanding of signs and wonders?
2. Have any of your ideas or attitudes changed during this study? How, and why?

This is early Wimber. He will show you how he feels about many years of simply hearing the Word in contrast to the way God has led him both to hear and do the Word.

13

Putting Theory Into Practice

by John Wimber

L earning how to pray for healing is like learning how to walk on water. In both areas it would be useful to know relevant biblical principles, to understand that Jesus is the Lord of all creation, to talk to others who have been successfully involved in the activity and to compare notes on why various approaches succeed or fail. All of this would be helpful. However, when the time came to "get out of the boat," all the best ideas and insights on "water walking" would be of little value.

The ability to transcend the laws of nature successfully is not discovered by mastering techniques or methodologies. When it comes to ministering in the power of the Holy Spirit many people know why certain things can or should happen. Fewer people actually see them happen in their own experience. In the evangelical community there are, in my opinion, two major obstacles to moving into the healing ministry.

Is Knowledge an End in Itself?

The first is the presupposition that knowledge is an end in itself. In the last forty years since the end of World War II, there has been a resurgence of Bible study. This emphasis has been brought about by the Holy Spirit who has brought renewal to the church. This move toward Bible study has been a positive and beneficial influence on the church worldwide. As with many good things, however, Bible study to an extreme can become an end in itself and result in an inundated or incomplete Christian experience.

It is not enough to be students of the Word only. In many circles knowledge gained by this means becomes the mark of the "elite." These "spiritually elite ones" have the ability to give the latest in eschatological forecasting and interpretation; they have the ability to quote large sections of Scripture and to discuss the nuances of the "latest teachings."

What pastor hasn't had a parishioner come and say, "I would like to get into an in-depth Bible study with the meat of the Word." These encounters often will occur immediately after the pastor has preached. This not only impugns the pastor but reinforces a belief in the frothiness of his own serving. The parishioner is unaware of this and is simply responding to a group programming which has conditioned him or her to believe that spiritual depth can be acquired in the "classroom."

Actually, nothing is further from the truth. If you want the meat of the Word, you can find it by encountering the world and giving them the gospel. The meat is in the street. People who want to grow in their Christian acumen must do so by exercising the Word of God in real situations which requires risk taking. James has said, "Be doers of the Word and not hearers only."

Knowing and Doing

A second major obstacle is the assumption that if we know something we have arrived at the apex, because to know is the highest goal.

Our Christian experience for the most part has become a cerebral exercise in which we have been conditioned to give intellectual assent to the truths of Scripture. I am not saying that this is a sterile environment in which we do not have any emotional or social interaction, but that our emphasis has been primarily intellectual assent to a given body of truths.

The difficulty with this Christian posture is that when we encounter real tests of faith we are unprepared. To illustrate this, let me take you out of the theological arena and apply it to skydiving. We assemble weekly to hear someone lecture on the great skydivers of the past, both the old and the new. The speaker shares the original language in an attempt to clarify every nuance of technique, methodology and experience of these great skydivers. After several months of this "classroom work" we are brought up front and given a certificate of graduation that declares we are now skydivers. Then a pupil asks, "When do we put on a parachute and jump?"

That is the moment of truth from which many students of skydiving—as well as students of the Word of God—shy away. But there must be application and exercise of the Word. At some time you must jump and grab the ripcord.

Please hear me carefully. The study of the Word is absolutely essential to the Christian life but *hearing without doing is incomplete*. Learning to walk in the Holy Spirit, learning to do the things the apostles did, is not an interesting alternative or option to Christian experience. It is the very commandment of God.

How Jesus Taught

Remember that some of the last recorded words of Jesus are those which He voiced in Matthew 28:19f. He told His disciples that all power had been given to Him and that they should make their move accordingly: "Go therefore and make disciples of all the nations, baptizing them in the name of the Father and the Son and the Holy Spirit, teaching them to observe all that I have commanded you...."

A part of what He commanded was to heal the sick (Luke 10:1-11).

The apostles had some difficulty learning to follow Jesus and the miraculous. They had difficulty in understanding the teachings of Jesus (Matt. 13:36; 15:15; 16:6-12). They had difficulty with the purpose of Jesus' mission (Mark 8:31-32; 9:31-32). They misunderstood His authority as it related to the kingdom of God (Mark 10:35-40; Luke 9:46-48).

The apostles throughout the ministry of Jesus were in a learning environment. They were not only learning new ideas but developing new skills and abilities. Even a superficial examination of the Gospels would demonstrate that they were on a learning curve. Failure characterized the early attempts of all the apostles to minister (Luke 9:37-43,52-55), but in the life of Peter these are more easily documented. One example is Peter's abortive attempt to walk on water (Matt. 14:11-33).

Feeding the 5,000

Certainly one of the greatest miracles in the New Testament is the feeding of the 5,000. Often when we read this text, we read it in a vacuum, never having experienced the performing of the miraculous ourselves. Therefore, our interpretation is controlled by that limitation. But those of us who have performed the miraculous read these kinds of texts with a different insight.

Look at Mark 6:33-44. Notice five things about this story. First, the compassion of Jesus (vs. 34). This compassion was not limited to a human response. This compassion is a supernatural gift—the gift of mercy. Often it precipitated the works of Jesus. Moved with compassion, He healed (Mark 1:41; Matt. 20:33) and taught (Mark 6:34). Moved with compassion, He performed miracles (Mark 8:2-10; Luke 7:11-17) and raised the dead (Luke 7:12-15). Moved with compassion, He healed the demonized (Mark 5:19). Compassion often precipitates the mighty works of God.

Second, notice (vs. 35-36) that the apostles observed the hungry condition of the crowd, the lack of immediate resource, and at that point came up with the suggestion of dispersing the crowd. All of this was handled on an entirely human and natural level with no thought of the miraculous. If Jesus had acceded to their suggestion, one of the greatest miracles in the history of the Bible would have been lost. I wonder how many times we have naturally disposed of things in the church that could have been an occasion for the miraculous.

Third, upon hearing the apostles' suggestion, Jesus responds with one of the most profound statements in Scripture (vs. 37-38), "You give them something to eat."

This, of course, caused the apostles to reexamine their resources: five loaves and two fish! Have you ever felt like that? So many to feed, so little to feed them with. Until you become a doer of the Word, you will never identify with the helpless feelings that the apostles had at that moment. Until you have stood before a blind person and commanded the eyes to see, you will not know the feeling of total inadequacy that comes when you look into yourself to accomplish this miracle. But therein is the crucible in which faith is formed. It is in this kind of activity that faith is evidence.

Organization and Faith

The fourth point I want to make is that Jesus gave instructions (vs. 39-40) to organize the crowd, and the apostles immediately did so. Now it is one thing to set the table for thousands of hungry people knowing you have food. It is quite another thing to do it wondering where you are going to get the food. Anyone who has ever committed himself or herself to praying for the sick understands these principles. Week after week one gets ready for encounters with the sick, knowing that if God does not show up, nothing will happen.

My fifth point (vs. 41) is that many commentators believe that the miracle of multiplication occurred in the hands of Jesus. They may be right! But having been a participant in the working of miracles, I'm sure that it could well have happened in the hands of the apostles. I am not saying that they could work miracles. Only God can do that. What I am saying is that often they occur in the hands of the person God is using.

Therefore, I believe that the apostles were handed, after the blessing, a meager portion of bread and fish. Then they had to step out into the crowd and begin passing that out, and the multiplication occurred right before their eyes. Since Scripture is somewhat obscure at this point, it is difficult to argue this position. But even so, I believe the miracle is in your hands and heart, and multiplication will come through you.

We must do better than the apostles did in "learning" this. Mark summarizes this for us in 6:52: "And they were utterly astonished, for they had not gained any insight from the incident of the loaves, but their heart was hardened." Even after they had, in conjunction with Jesus, worked this mighty miracle, they still did not understand.

The obstacles then to entering a healing ministry are twofold: 1) the study of the Bible as an end in itself, and 2) a cerebral exercise of Christianity.

Now that we have seen these, let's turn to the question which often is raised: "How can I overcome these obstacles?" I think the answer is a change of worldview.

Worldview Adjustments

The scope of this article will allow us to deal only with the surface issues of worldview with a hope of whetting appetites to study and experience the issue further. James Sire (*The Universe Next Door*, Inter-Varsity Press) says, "A worldview is a set of presuppositions (or assumptions) which we hold (consciously or subconsciously) about the basic makeup of our world."

A more technical definition is given by Charles Kraft in his book, *Christianity in Culture*: "Cultures pattern perceptions of reality into conceptualizations of what reality can or should be, what is to be regarded as actual, probable, possible or impossible. These conceptualizations form what is termed the "worldview" of our culture. The worldview is the central systemization of conceptions of reality to which the members of its culture assent (largely unconsciously) and from which stems their value system. The worldview lies at the very heart of the culture, touching, interacting with, and strongly influencing every aspect of the culture" (p. 53).

Both authors are saying the same thing. Their point is that the starting points from which we view things differ. Even though we may possess the same reasoning process, we end up with different conclusions. This process is basically a learned process. A worldview is imposed on us as youth by means of teaching.

An illustration of this would be to ask ourselves the questions: On what do we focus? How do we see or conceive of reality?

We do not see everything we look at. We are selective. The media occasionally reports people being injured by the explosion of an "empty" gas container. We have been taught that the can is empty because there is no fluid in it. That is what our focus is on. We do not see that the can is full of gas fumes so we light a match and *boom!* We accept that which confirms what we have been taught and usually reject what contradicts what we have been taught.

What Happened at Lystra?

Look at Acts 14:8-18 and you can see this "taught focus" occurring. This passage records the event of Paul and Barnabas healing a lame man in Lystra. A commotion arose on account of this event. The people of Lystra had a basic assumption, a starting point which helped them arrive at a conclusion which for them was "reality." Their assumption was that only the gods could effect such a healing. Therefore, when they saw what had happened, their conclusion was that Paul and Barnabas were gods for which they had no names. They began to worship and offer sacrifices to them. On the other hand, Paul and Barnabas's basic assumption was that they were only carrying out what they were commissioned by Christ to do: heal the sick, bring the rule of God into the world. The starting point assures a certain conclusion (Kraft, p. 57).

Dealing with one's worldview and going through a "paradigm shift" is sometimes extremely painful. Still, it may have to happen in order for one to operate with a New Testament healing model. A "paradigm" is defined by Webster as an example or pattern. A "shift" indicates moving from one model or pattern to another. This begins as a mental process and ends as an experience. Thus the overcoming of the obstacles mentioned above begins with the process of changing one's worldview.

A question I am often asked is, "How can I make such a change?" If you wish to begin to view reality from a different set of assumptions here are at least three ways to get started.

1. Investigate alternative worldviews by:
   a. *Reading books.* There are at least two you can start with: Charles Kraft, *Christianity and Culture*, Orbis Books, Maryknoll, New York (a seminary level text); and James Sire, *The Universe Next Door*, Inter-Varsity Press, Downers Grove, Illinois, 1976 (written in

143

popular style).

    b. Read "The Flaw of the Excluded Middle" by Paul Hiebert, in *Missiology: An International Review*; American Society of Missiology, Elkhart, Indiana, Vol. X, No. 1, January 1982 (pp. 35-47).

    c. Take a course which would deal with the issue at a Bible college or seminary.

2. Find a church whose worldview observes and includes a healing ministry. (Remember there are many models in this arena.)

3. Start where you are, praying for the sick. (The books found in the "Recommended Books for Reading" list are an excellent place to secure information.)

DISCUSSION QUESTIONS

1. Why is "Bible study to an extreme" so potentially hazardous? How can this be avoided?

2. Have you ever met someone who appeared to feel he or she knew all there was to know about a particular subject? How did you react? How does this limit one in dealing with "real tests of faith," as Wimber mentioned? What is the best way to deal with someone such as this?

3. Do you agree that "hearing without doing is incomplete"? Consider this in view of James 2:17-26 and 3:13-18.

4. How do you feel about God doing the miraculous "through" you?

5. Are you prepared to go through a "paradigm shift," such as Wimber speaks of? How can this be accomplished? Are you willing to do what is necessary? Why or why not?

APPLICATION

If your group has considered all the options and feels led to begin a healing ministry, go back and review Chapter 3. Then look over the attitudes, assumptions and scriptures listed. Finally, spend time together praying for guidance and wisdom as you step out into this new aspect of faith.

For additional information and/or explanation, see the list of tapes and books in the bibliography.

Very few individuals have been used by God to the extent that John Wimber has been used in the 1980s to turn the thinking and ministry of fellow Christians toward the supernatural works of the Holy Spirit. In this final chapter, one of the newer professors at Fuller, British-born Eddie Gibbs, makes an up-to-date assessment of this extraordinary man of God.

14

My Friend, John Wimber
by Eddie Gibbs

An expert is described as "a person with a briefcase at least fifty miles away from home." On neither count does this apply to John Wimber. His "stuff," as he describes his material, does not come out of detached study but has arisen out of the challenges of local church ministry. And, unlike many globe-trotters who are better known on the international circuit than in their own neighborhood, John Wimber pastors a dynamic congregation which has spawned a nationwide movement.

The Vineyard fellowship in Anaheim, California, has grown to a weekly attendance of more than 5,000 meeting in a converted warehouse close by Disneyland. In addition it has planted many more new churches in Southern California and across the nation and welcomed other groups into its fellowship. Currently some 200 congregations identify with the Vineyard movement. So John is no fly-by-night, inflating his reputation by extravagant claims. He works from a home base church which also serves as a workshop and where he invites verification.

I first met John Wimber in 1979 when I was on a two-week visit to Fuller Seminary in Pasadena, California, to take Peter Wagner's intensive course in church growth as part of the doctor of ministry program. John gave some of the lectures, and his contribution, which made a great impression on me, was not in the area of "signs and wonders" but in the management of a large and growing church. He spoke with such practical wisdom and spiritual insight that I felt many churches in Britain could benefit greatly from his experience and expertise. I especially appreciated his gentleness, honesty and humility.

On the basis of that initial contact, I spoke to Bishop David Pytches of St. Andrew's, Chorleywood, where I was then worshipping, about the possibility of John's leading a church growth seminar for us.

Church Reaching Out

Two years later I was back at Fuller for the next phase of the D.Min. program, and this gave me the opportunity to pay my first visit to the Vineyard church, which then met in a gymnasium in Canyon High School. My friend, David Watson, a fellow British Anglican, was also in Pasadena, teaching the church renewal course, and I suggested that he should check out the Vineyard, as an example of a church reaching out into the community in effective evangelism as a fruit of their renewal. I could have had no idea at the time of the far-reaching consequences of that suggestion.

By the time John paid his visit to England for church growth ministry, the agenda had changed radically. Instead of coming to lecture on the management of a growing church, he came, with twenty-eight of his church members, to demonstrate the dynamics of a growing church through ministering in the reconciliation and healing power of the Holy Spirit.

During his first weekend at Chorleywood, I was conducting seminars in Durham and phoning Pastor David Pytches after every service to enquire what had happened and how people were reacting. Sadly, it's not often that one feels one is missing something significant when absent from a church service. But when John is around unexpected things are liable to happen. I say "unexpected" because, as author/psychologist John White observed at one of John's courses held at Fuller, "Manifestations of various kinds could be witnessed, though no attempt was made in the course to create or bring about such phenomena."

Having witnessed uninhibited physical and emotional

manifestations in a "laid-back" California setting, I was fascinated to see precisely the same phenomena occurring during John's meetings in the United Kingdom, among those who were sublimely ignorant of the way that they were expected to respond on such occasions!

Ongoing Ministry

Having known John for six years, visited his church on a number of occasions and sat through three of his "signs and wonders" courses here at Fuller, how do I now feel about his ministry?

I find him to be a person of great humility and personal integrity. He is ready to acknowledge that many people who are prayed for are not healed. Unlike some itinerant "healers," he does not ignore the hard cases but insists on an ongoing ministry to them. He does not attribute lack of healing to absence of faith on the part of the person being ministered to. Neither does he tell people to ignore their symptoms. When people ask, "Am I healed?" he counsels them to see their doctor.

Having ministered to individuals, John will then ask whether they feel any better or have noticed any change. If they answer in the negative this is taken as an indication of a need for further ministry. In the Vineyard fellowships this follow-up ministry may be in the form of ongoing care within one of the "kinship groups" which make up the committed membership of the church, or through one-to-one counseling sessions arranged with the pastoral staff.

I have heard people joke about those who visit the Vineyard, as scores do each week, that they are on a trip to "Wimberland." Such jocular remarks might give the impression that the church sustains itself exclusively on the manna of "signs and wonders." In fact, there is no undue emphasis on supernatural phenomena; the teaching is on a broadly based, biblical diet of faithful expository preaching. And the church stimulates an impressive range of social-concern ministries, including prison visitation, caring for the homes and needs of the elderly, and ministry among the poor in Mexico.

Some have been surprised by the news that John is no longer

teaching the "signs and wonders" course here at Fuller
Seminary and that the course was dropped from the curriculum
during the 1985-1986 academic year. People are concerned
about the reasons for its postponement, which are both political
and theological.

Victim of Success

Fuller Seminary is the second largest seminary in the United
States, with an enrollment of about 2,700 students, representing ninety denominations and more than seventy countries. The
course was offered by the School of World Mission, not only
to its own students but also to those of the other two schools
of theology and psychology. It soon became the victim of its
own success, which could more easily be contained within the
structures of a church setting than within a seminary. It was
difficult to arrange appropriate "workshop experience" and
provide ongoing pastoral care for a large student body, scattered around the greater Los Angeles area, maintaining their
studies by part-time work and looking to churches of all kinds
for pastoring.

Despite the problem it instantly became the most popular of
the 600 courses offered on campus, which already included
several courses on the work and gifts of the Spirit. Between 1982
and 1985, 800 students attended. Such was the demand that
guards had to be stationed at the doors to prevent gate-crashers.

Having attended one of the classes, the editor of *Christian
Life* magazine, an influential periodical read by a wide spectrum of the evangelical church leadership, dedicated the entire
October 1982 issue of the magazine to "signs and wonders,"
with the words "MC510 COULD CHANGE YOUR LIFE!
across the cover. (MC510 is the catalog reference for the course
taught by John Wimber and C. Peter Wagner.)

Fuller Seminary's Diversity

Widespread publicity continued to the point that the non-
charismatic evangelical community became alarmed, wondering whether Fuller was becoming Pentecostal. In reality, it is
estimated that about thirty percent of the student body would
identify with the charismatic movement, but only nine percent

come from Pentecostal or charismatic churches or denominations that adhere to Pentecostal or charismatic movements. By far the largest contingent is Presbyterians, with Baptists coming a distant second. This diversity is also represented in the full-time faculty of the three schools, drawn from twenty-five denominations and a wide range of evangelical, theological opinion.

It must also be realized that John served as one of a large number of adjunct professors who are called in to teach courses in their specialist area, and was never a full-time faculty person. Therefore Peter Wagner, who invited John to teach at Fuller, served as the professor of record for the course.

In addition to expressions of concern by church spokesmen unsympathetic to the charismatic emphasis in any form, there were those within the seminary who became disturbed by some of the reports they were hearing from a small minority of students who had reacted negatively to the course. Questions were therefore raised in the School of Theology which demanded serious consideration.

Different Perspective

The School of Theology's perspective was inevitably different from that of the School of World Mission, which had originated the course in response to the needs of its 600 students, made up of established church leaders from the Two-Thirds World, missionaries taking in-service training, and pre-service personnel. For the great majority of these people, the world of the supernatural and the demonic was a fact of life rather than a subject for debate, with many of the overseas Christians having been converted to Christianity from other religions as a result of some form of "power encounter." When people from the Two-Thirds World come to the West for post-graduate theological education, the programs they are offered must meet the needs they will face and the customs which arise from their cross-cultural context.

Although John Wimber had never been a missionary, he had undergone a significant shift in worldview perspective, which enabled him to begin to address the issues with which our students from overseas were having to grapple. He, therefore, came as a pioneer, not only to teach the student body but to articulate and demonstrate ministry in the power of the Holy Spirit in the presence of the School of World Mission faculty, who did have the anthropological and missiological insights to translate his concepts and ministry models into a cross-cultural setting.

Unanimous Backing

The twelve-member faculty of the School of World Mission is concerned to address the issue of power evangelism, because they are convinced of its crucial importance for the furtherance of the gospel worldwide.

We of the School of World Mission faculty did not feel, however, able to proceed further until the course had been re-examined both theologically, psychologically and pastorally. Many of the questions which had been raised in the School of Theology had also been raised in the School of World Mission.

Through conversations with John, I know that he too is looking for answers in a number of these areas. The course was therefore postponed for one year, simply to allow time for more adequate communication and evaluation. The aim was not to produce a watered-down, but an improved, version in this highly sensitive area of experimental theology, applicable not only to missiology but also theology and psychology.

Questions Raised

Here are some of the questions raised here at Fuller and elsewhere.

1. Is the ministry of healing primarily to provide answers to medical problems, or is it to be understood as a sign of the present reality of the kingdom of God? Do I presuppose that it is God's intention to heal everyone, or is miraculous healing an occasional intervention which can neither be predicted nor commanded, so that there is always an element of surprise and a recognition of God's sovereign intervention?

2. Does the ministry of Jesus as recorded in the Gospels provide a paradigm for Christian ministry in later centuries?

152

Are the signs which attended our Lord's ministry intended to confirm His unique Sonship and Messiahship, or do they characterize the ministry of every Spirit-filled person through whom the present reality of the kingdom is to be demonstrated?

3. Is there an undue triumphalism in John Wimber's teaching? How does he respond to the fact that, despite our redemption, we continue as part of a creation which "groans in travail" until it attains its full redemption? How are we to combine an experiential knowledge of "the power of the resurrection" with "the fellowship of His sufferings" which emphasizes that the pathway of our pilgrimage leads through death to life?

4. Does John open himself to criticism by too readily testifying to specific instances of healing without adequate evidence that a claimed healing was either valid or sustained?

5. What influence can demons have over the lives of believers? If a believer is a "temple of the Holy Spirit," can he/she at the same time be oppressed or even inhabited by demons?

6. What is John's theological explanation for healing being withheld from a person who has come in faith to receive the ministry of healing? How do we minister pastorally to such a person when, following the ministry for healing, his or her physical or mental condition continues to deteriorate?

7. Is there a causal relationship between "signs and wonders" and effective evangelism? How do we balance the accounts of widespread response in the Gospels and Acts with wholesale rejection in Capernaum and Chorazim, where such phenomena had been a regular occurrence? Is the twentieth-century secular humanist as likely to be impressed by "signs and wonders" as a first-century observer?

8. What is our response to mature believers from the Two-Thirds World, for whom the existence of the demonic and

the reality of "signs and wonders" is a fact of life rather than a subject for debate? Do we accept their worldview as being objectively valid? Are we prepared to learn from their insights? If Christians accept a Western worldview and consider that their own understanding has greater objective validity, how can they avoid theological education from becoming secularizing?

Primary Issue: Doers of the Word

These are tough questions which I am certain will be debated over the years to come. The primary question, however, is what becomes of ministry to those in need while the debate remains unresolved? Inevitably we must continue to teach the importance of the power of the Spirit and the gifts of the Spirit, as we have always done. I would suggest that our practice must continue alongside our theorizing. By so doing it will provide fresh data to stimulate our theologizing just as our theological reflection will continue to control and refine our practice. Are we not, after all, called to be doers as well as hearers of the Word?

In the "doing" we each fulfill different functions in the body of Christ. A healing ministry is at its strongest in the setting of the ongoing, worshipping community. Some, as in the case of John Wimber, will have an extraordinary gift of faith which will eventually stimulate the God-given gifts in others. Alongside will be those who, while exercising discernment, will be maintaining a level of detachment and asking the hard questions. Hopefully, this will not be out of a predisposition to unbelief, but out of a regard for truth. Both approaches are necessary functions in the body, providing the needed stimuli, checks and balances.

Personally, I have never, to my knowledge, been used in a ministry of instantaneous healing, but I am thankful for having been a close observer, which stance has caused me to wonder, in both senses of that word. I have both "wondered," rejoicing at what God has done, as well as "wondered" in perplexity as I have struggled with unanswered theological, missiological, psychological and pastoral questions.

EDDIE GIBBS *moved from England to Pasadena, California, in 1983 to assume his teaching ministry at Fuller. He holds the D.Min. degree in church growth.*

DISCUSSION QUESTIONS

1. Eddie Gibbs points out that Christians from the Third World have a special need for ministering with the power of signs and wonders. Is this also true in some places and among some groups in North America? How about Europe?
2. Do you feel that miraculous healing is a fact of life rather than a subject of debate?
3. Gibbs says he has not been used for miraculous healing. Have you? Have you seen it up close? Do you wish God to use you in that way?
4. Do you think believers can be oppressed or possessed by demons?
5. Why is it that God heals some and not others?

APPLICATION

Form a Bible study group or find an existing one which would be willing to discuss each one of Gibbs's questions over a period of a month or two. Ask the leader to prepare a study with key biblical texts for each one.

Bibliography

RECOMMENDED BOOKS AND TAPES ON HEALING

Bridge, Donald. *Signs and Wonders Today.* Leicester, England: Inter-Varsity Press, 1985. 204 pp.

Bubeck, Mark I. *The Adversary: The Christian Versus Demon Activity.* Chicago: Moody, 1975. 158 pp.

Cassidy, Michael. *Bursting the Wineskins.* Wheaton, Ill.: Harold Shaw, 1983. 256 pp.

Harper, Michael. *Spiritual Warfare: Recognizing and Overcoming the Work of Evil Spirits.* Ann Arbor, Mich.: Servant Books, 1984.

Kelsey, Morton T. *Healing and Christianity.* San Francisco: Harper & Row, 1973. 359 pp.

Lawrence, Roy. *Christian Healing Rediscovered: A Guide to Spiritual, Mental, Physical Wholeness.* Downers Grove, Ill.: Inter-Varsity Press, 1980. 128 pp.

MacNutt, Francis. *Healing.* Notre Dame: Ave Maria Press, 1974.

Mallone, George. *Those Controversial Gifts.* Downers Grove, Ill.: Inter-Varsity Press, 1983. 154 pp.

Ogilvie, Lloyd John. *Why Not? Accept Christ's Healing and Wholeness.* Old Tappan, N.J.: Fleming Revell, 1985. 190 pp.

Sanford, Agnes. *The Healing Light.* St. Paul, Minn.: Macalester Park Publishing Co., 1947. 168 pp.

Wagner, C. Peter. *Spiritual Power and Church Growth.* Altamonte Springs, Fla.: Creation House, 1986.

Wimber, John. *Power Evangelism.* San Francisco: Harper & Row, 1986.

Wimber, John. *Power Healing.* San Francisco: Harper & Row, 1987.

SIGNS AND WONDERS TODAY

Wright, Gordon. *In Quest of Healing* Springfield, Mo · Gospel
Publishing House, 1984 160 pp

TAPES

John Wimber: Signs, Wonders and Church Growth—Part I; Signs,
Wonders and Church Growth—Part II. Available from Vineyard
Ministries International, P.O. Box 65004, Anaheim, CA 92805.

Index

159

Index

Walker, Jim, 128-129
Walker, Robert, 4
Wallis, Jim, 33
Wang, David, 47-48, 82-87
Warfield, Benjamin, 110
Watson, David, 80, 148
Wesley, John, 60, 61, 63
Wheaton College, 115
White, John, 148
Widdecombe, Malcolm, 81
Wilson, Rev., 73
Wimber, Carol, 41
Wimber, John, 3-11, 14, 39-49, 80, 108-109, 111,
    116, 127, 128, 130, 132-133, 137-145, 147-155,
    157-158
worldview, 21-22, 29, 142-143
word of knowledge, 40, 121, 125-127
worship, 30-31
Wright, Gordon, 158
Wright, Nigel, 81

Y

Young, Don, 97-100
Youth With a Mission, 79

Z

Zimbabwe, 103
Zone, Enrique, 97
Zulus, 101-102

NOTES

NOTES

NOTES

NOTES

NOTES

NOTES

NOTES